Wakefield Press

FLIGHT TO FAME

Peter Monteath is Professor of History at Flinders University,
where he teaches and writes about modern Australian and European history.
He is also President of the History Council of South Australia and
a trustee of the History Trust of South Australia.

Portrait of Ross Smith in flight gear, approx. 1920.
[Ross and Keith Smith Collection, SLSA PRG 18/53/2]

FLIGHT TO FAME

VICTORY IN THE 1919 GREAT AIR RACE,
ENGLAND TO AUSTRALIA

SIR ROSS SMITH

EDITED AND INTRODUCED BY
PETER MONTEATH

FOREWORD BY
AIR CHIEF MARSHAL SIR ANGUS HOUSTON,
AK, AFC (RET'D)

Wakefield
Press

Wakefield Press
16 Rose Street
Mile End
South Australia 5031
www.wakefieldpress.com.au

14,000 Miles Through the Air first published 1922
This edition published 2019

Cover designed by Liz Nicholson, Wakefield Press
Text designed and typeset by Michael Deves, Wakefield Press

ISBN 978 1 74305 640 0

A catalogue record for this
book is available from the
National Library of Australia

Wakefield Press thanks
Coriole Vineyards for
continued support

Contents

View of the Vickers Vimy crew, James Bennett, Ross Smith, Keith Smith,
and Walter Shiers, standing by the Vickers Vimy G-EAOU after arriving in
Darwin, the final stage of the England–Australia air race.
[Ross and Keith Smith Collection, SLSA PRG 18/9/3/2a]

Foreword

AIR CHIEF MARSHAL SIR ANGUS HOUSTON,
AK, AFC (RET'D)

All Australians need to know more about the wonderful achievement of Sir Ross Smith, Sir Keith Smith and flight engineers Wally Shiers and Jim Bennett in conducting the first flight from London (Hounslow) to Darwin, Australia in 1919. This year, 100 years after their historic flight we commemorate that success.

Peter Monteath should be commended for reviewing and editing Ross Smith's original manuscript published by Macmillan in 1922. He also deserves praise for his complete and comprehensive introduction to *Flight to Fame* as it provides important context and essential background for the reader.

A century after the epic flight it is difficult to comprehend what a great achievement it was. In this modern era we can board a Qantas Dreamliner in London and fly non-stop in complete comfort and safety to Perth in all weathers in about 17 hours. It has become routine.

In contrast, Sir Ross and his crew flew their Vickers Vimy from London to Darwin for 18000 kilometres in 136 hours of flying over 24 sectors in 28 days, often landing and taking off from unsuitable and dangerous airfields, horse racing tracks, jungle clearings and desert strips.

The challenge was immense.

The risk was extreme.

The Vimy was a twin engine biplane with an open cockpit with no protection from the elements for the crew. With rudimentary navigation instruments, very basic flight instruments and no auto-pilot, artificial horizon or anti-icing equipment, only an experienced, skilled and determined pilot and crew could have handled the challenge and managed the risks of this pioneering flight.

Sir Ross Smith was a remarkable man who joined the 3rd Light Horse at the outbreak of war in 1914. He fought at Gallipoli and in the Middle East at the Battle of Romani. After joining Number 1 Squadron, Australian Flying Corps, he demonstrated great courage and skill in the air shooting down 11 enemy aircraft in the Middle East. His bravery and inspirational wartime service on the ground and in the air was recognised with the award of a Military Cross and bar and a Distinguished Flying Cross and two bars. In his book *Seven Pillars of Wisdom* Lawrence of Arabia describes Ross Smith as 'an Australian of a race delighting in additional risks'.

In this highly readable book about the epic flight, Sir Ross Smith describes how he and his crew demonstrated great skill, tenacity, endurance and improvisation to overcome every challenge on the 'Flight to Fame'.

Air Chief Marshal Sir Angus Houston, AK, AFC (Ret'd)
Patron, Epic Flight Centenary

Sir Ross and Sir Keith Smith's arrival from England at Northfield.
The race from England to Australia was won on their arrival at Darwin.
The crew later flew the plane from Darwin to Adelaide arriving at Northfield.
The photograph shows the biplane about to land in the scrub at Northfield.
[SLSA B 7967]

Ross Smith (pilot) and Mustard (rear gunner) in their Bristol F.2 B fighter, part
of No. 1 Squadron, Australian Flying Corps, serving in the Middle East, c. 1917.
[Ross and Keith Smith Collection, SLSA PRG 18/4/19]

Introduction

PETER MONTEATH

In September 1916, the South Australian Light Horseman Ross Macpherson Smith wrote from Egypt to his mother in Adelaide that he was trying to get into the Flying Corps. 'I want excitement and to feel that I am doing something' he told her. 'It may be a trifle more dangerous than this job, but I can't help liking risky jobs. The same thing in me that made me take on bombing and then machine-guns is now asking for flying. You would not wish it otherwise, would you?'[1]

Smith was a member of a generation characterised by a form of gallantry bordering on the casual. Yet in his case, it pushed him to achievements which marked him as a giant among his peers. Having survived more than four months in the hell of Gallipoli, Smith's appetite for risk had seen him join a machine-gun battalion in the Light Horse. No matter what his mother might have thought of the idea of her son taking to the skies, he carried through with his dream of fighting his war in and from the air. And when that war was over, Smith's irrepressible spirit of adventure persuaded him to take on a flight which at that moment in history appeared absurdly ambitious. Just 16 years after the Wright brothers had defied gravity for precious seconds, Smith would pilot an aircraft from England all the way to his Antipodean homeland, and then on to his home town of Adelaide.

This book is Ross Smith's own account of that journey, undertaken with three other Australians in a Vickers Vimy bomber. Penned in the months that followed their historic flight, and as the Smith brothers and their two mechanics Wally Shiers and Jim Bennett basked in the fame that their feat of sustained daring had brought them, the book was published in 1922. It offers its readers insights into the perils confronting the pioneers of flight. More than that, it reveals the character of all those men and women who, like Smith, could not help but take on 'risky jobs', and who all too often paid the highest price.

ROSS SMITH, WAR HERO

Born in Semaphore in 1892, Ross Smith was educated at Queen's School in North Adelaide, and for a couple of years at Warriston School in his parents' native Scotland. He spent a good part of his early life on a massive property in South Australia's north-east, near the rail line connecting Port Pirie with Broken Hill. 'Mutooroo' was managed by Ross's Scottish-born father Andrew, who won plaudits for his achievements in running thousands of sheep over the parched expanses.

When war broke out, Ross abandoned his storeman's job at Harris Scarfe to enlist with the Light Horse and sailed for Egypt on the first of the convoys to leave South Australia in October 1914. He was not among those sent to Gallipoli for the landing on 25 April the following year, but from Egypt he followed the course of the battle and could barely wait to join it. He wrote to his mother on 7 May that 'an Australian with my blood is good enough for any six Turks. The Old Highland blood in me rises high when I think of the days to come and I'll keep my end up all right'.[2] At Gallipoli he certainly

Cabinet card studio portrait of Ross Smith, aged approximately eighteen months, 1893. [Ross and Keith Smith Collection, SLSA PRG 18/1/2]

Portrait of Ross (left), Colin (centre), and Keith (right) Smith, 1906.
Colin, the youngest, was killed on the Western Front in 1917.
[Ross and Keith Smith Collection, SLSA PRG 18/1/10]

did, receiving his baptism of fire in vicious fighting in mid-May and spending the best part of his Dardanelles tour of duty in trenches. Fortunately he was held in reserve at Quinn's Post at the time of the bloody and ill-executed assault on Turkish positions. Reflecting later on his Gallipoli experience, he wrote that his months there

> were quite happy ones and full of fun. The tucker certainly could have been improved upon, but then 'War is War' isn't it, and not all beer and skittles? One soon gets used to doing with only a few hours' sleep a day, but I never want to try and do 11 days and night again with only about 30 hours sleep the whole time. As far as the bullets go, one treats them with contempt, and never thinks of being hit.

By October he was *en route* to England via the islands of Lemnos and Imbros and then Gibraltar to recover from a severe bout of typhoid. Only after five restless months was he able to return to the Light Horse in Egypt in April 1916, entering a desert camp between Zeitoun and Heliopolis. By that time most of the AIF was already in France, while the Middle East slipped down the priorities of the British government. Nonetheless, the military situation there was precarious, as Turkish forces threatened to push westward into Egypt. By May, Smith had been recalled to his regiment and placed in charge of a machine-gun section, where his dedication and efficiency earned him a promotion to First Lieutenant. In August, nearly a year since he had last seen action at Gallipoli, the Battle of Romani provided a bitter taste of desert warfare, in which the two sides threw at each other all of the machine-gun fire they could muster. He told his mother:

It's a marvel to me now that I was not killed a dozen times a day. I've forgotten what fear is (at least at a time like that), and when I saw those Turks out in front of my gun, it seemed the most natural thing in the world to walk out there and shoot them, and it never occurred to me that they might possibly get me ... Such is War. It's a feeling (and to me a delightful one) that I defy anyone to express. I felt absolutely bursting with life and energy, and I've never felt so vitally alive before as on that morning, and, above all, there was a burning desire to kill.

As he had anticipated to his mother, it was in October 1916 that Ross Smith took the life-changing step of joining the Australian Flying Corps. Australia was the only one of the British Dominions to have its own Flying Corps; what was initially No. 67 (Australian) Squadron in the Royal Flying Corps became No. 1 Squadron, Australian Flying Corps. For its continued existence the Corps relied heavily on aeroplanes and equipment supplied by the British, while the Australians provided men of the quality of Ross Smith, drawn commonly from the Light Horse, with a passion for flight and for combat, along with an almost cheerful disregard for the perils of war in the air.

Trained and deployed for six months as an observer, Smith then made the transition to the role of pilot. It was a step which offered relief from the inaction to which life in the Light Horse had returned, and it introduced him to the most advanced military technology of the day. Ironically, it also offered an opportunity to engage in the most old-fashioned form of warfare, namely man-to-man combat. One of his many brushes with death took the form of a dog-fight with a German in the skies over Weli Sheikl

Nuran. The two aircraft almost collided. When he crash-landed his BE12a at his home base, Smith had blood streaming from bullet wounds to his cheek and the top of his head.[3] It was the kind of bravery that would earn him multiple awards and distinctions. In under two years as an airman he gained the Military Cross, a bar to the Military Cross, and then a Distinguished Flying Cross, to which two bars were added. In the last three months of the war alone he won three decorations.[4]

One man who witnessed the combative spirit of Smith and other Australians was T.E. Lawrence – 'Lawrence of Arabia'. In *The Seven Pillars of Wisdom* he recalls an occasion when, while visiting a desert camp, an enemy aircraft appeared overhead: 'Our Australians, scrambling wildly to their yet-hot machines, started them in a moment. Ross Smith, with his observer, leaped into one, and climbed like a cat up the sky.' The Australians, Lawrence believed, 'were of a race delighting in additional risks', and from the safety of the ground he watched in awe as a drama unfolded in the skies above:

> Ross Smith fastened on the big one, and, after five minutes of sharp machine-gun rattle, the German dived suddenly towards the railway line. As it flashed behind the low ridge, there broke out a pennon of smoke, and from its falling place a soft, dark cloud. An 'Ah!' came from the Arabs about us. Five minutes later Ross Smith was back, and jumped gaily out of his machine, swearing that the Arab front was the place.[5]

When he was not engaged in combat, Smith was making reconnaissance flights over enemy territory and became the first 'British' airman to fly over and photograph Jerusalem.[6] On one such flight his passenger was the Australian war photographer Frank

Ross Smith in hospital, c. 1918, with his head heavily bandaged.
[Ross and Keith Smith Collection, SLSA PRG 18/5/20f]

Hurley, whose diary conveyed something of the romance of flight at that time:

> Oh, the exhilaration of that upward climb! The powerful throb of the engine whilst on the ground now resolved itself into a whirr, and the hangars rapidly decreased in size until they became mere specks. Up, up, we go – 1000, 2000, 3000, 4000 are indicated on the gauge and still we climb heavenward. The earth below is assuming the appearance of a patchwork. Here and there numerous villages are scattered . . . the roads radiate from them like white ribbons, the streams and wadies might be arteries with networks of veins. Long since, traffic on the road has converted itself into mote-like specks and still we climb heavenward.
>
> [. . .] We are crossing the hills of Judea at 90 miles per hour and yet from our great height we appear stationary. Away on the horizon lies a dark streak which is rapidly enlarging. It is the Dead Sea. In a few minutes we are over it and gliding down in volplane (at 100 miles an hour). I am powerless and utterly incapable of describing the wild and tremendous grandeur of the view now stretched before us. We are over enemy territory and they are firing at us with their 'archies'. Wretched shooting, to which we pay no attention. One is too absorbed in contemplation, in fact intoxicated by the mighty works of nature, to heed the vile endeavours of Turkish rabble to shoot us down. From the ground, we appear as a tiny humming bird flitting through the infinity of cloudless blue; from my seat, we are hurtling along on the wings of a tornado, poised over the deep blue waters of the Mystic Sea![7]

At Jenin aerodrome, 21 September 1918, the day after its capture.
Left to right: Ross Smith; Lt Campbell, AIF photographer; Lt Gullet, AIF war
correspondent; Cpl Luxton; and Gullet's driver with a captured drum.

Gullet is holding a bottle of champagne 'of which we had numerous mug-fulls during the day!' [Ross and Keith Smith Collection, SLSA PRG 18/4/4]

ENGLAND TO AUSTRALIA

By the end of the war Smith was one of the most respected and experienced of airmen, having clocked up some 600 hours as a pilot. Yet the conclusion of hostilities confronted him with the dilemma faced by so many others – what kind of career could he make for himself when the guns had fallen silent, and how would he return to his homeland?

Once again it was aviation that pointed the way. Such was the esteem in which Smith was held by British authorities that he was chosen to fly as a co-pilot on a survey flight to India. Brigadier-General A.E. 'Biffy' Borton had flown the latest Handley Page bomber from England to Egypt towards the end of the war, with the idea that it be deployed for night bombing raids. When the survey of possible air routes eastward to India and beyond was planned after the war, Borton opted for Ross Smith as his co-pilot. Aboard also were two Australian mechanics, Wally Shiers and Jim Bennett. As they commenced their flight from Cairo to Calcutta on 29 November, their goal was to plot an air route connecting Britain with its Indian Empire, identifying appropriate air-fields and refueling points along the way.

From Calcutta Borton chartered a ship to survey a further route on to Australia, taking Ross Smith with him as staff-captain. In making the survey, *Sphinx* carried fuel to distribute at points on the way, fuel which might serve the later needs of an aircraft bound for Australia. When the fuel ignited, the vessel was almost completely destroyed, and Smith and Borton were fortunate to escape with their lives. The replacement vessel *Minto* carried no fuel supplies but managed at least to deliver its airmen-surveyors safely to Koepang in Timor – within aerial striking distance of Australia –

before returning them to Calcutta for their flight to London.

At around this time politicians and military authorities were addressing the questions of how Anzac soldiers might be repatriated, and how the technology of flight, which had advanced at dizzying pace during the war, might serve to draw together even more closely the many parts of Britain's Empire, basking in the glow of victory in Europe.

One of them was the Australian Prime Minister Billy Hughes, who in early 1919 was splitting his time between Britain and France, as he strove to extract the best possible peace deal for Australia. Aware of the eagerness among Anzacs to return home, he was moved in March to consider a daring proposition. It was prompted, it seems, by a visit in Britain to demobilized soldiers, among them a number of airmen keen to fly their machines all the way to Australia. A substantial prize, Hughes was persuaded, could be offered to anyone who succeeded in such an enterprise. He suggested that such an undertaking 'would be a great advertisement for Australia and would concentrate the eyes of the world on us'.[8]

To put things in perspective, at that time no-one had yet flown across an ocean, let alone manage the 18000 kilometres to the Antipodes. Moreover, it was not at all clear where pilots would land their aircraft, given that even with a full load of fuel the ranges of most did not extend beyond several hundred kilometres. The planes would need to negotiate snow-capped mountain peaks, jungles, deserts and expansive bodies of water. Navigation instruments at that time were little more than a helpful adjunct to the crew's naked eyes – weather permitting. In parts of Asia east of India the landing strips would still need to be built to receive the intrepid aviators or some kind of makeshift alternative found. To complete a flight across half the world would require not just the most advanced machines the infant industry had at its disposal, but more than a dose of courage and good fortune.

Whatever reservations his Cabinet colleagues and others might have had, Hughes's idea was made known to the world on 19 March, albeit with the proviso that the exact rules were still to be announced. That happened in May. The rules developed by the Royal Aero Club made it clear that all aircraft entered in the race were to be privately financed and British made. Each team had to be comprised solely of Australians; one crew member had to be a qualified navigator. All had to forfeit any claim for loss or injury. The extraordinarily handsome £10,000 prize would remain open from September 1919 until the end of that year, by which time the winning team would have needed to fly from the Hounslow airfield in London and land in Darwin no more than 30 days later.[9]

THE GREAT AIR RACE

A list of those who considered entering the Great Air Race reads something like a 'Who's Who' of early Australian aviation. It also shows how closely interwoven the history of aviation was with the Great War. The first tentative entry of all was received from Queenslander Bert Hinkler, who during the war had served with the Royal Naval Service in Belgium and France, earning himself a Distinguished Service Medal before being posted as a pilot to a squadron operating in Italy. Hinkler's problem was that the race rules expressly forbade solo flights, as the presence of a navigator was considered essential. He was obliged to withdraw his entry at that time, but a decade later he became the first pilot to make a solo flight from England to Australia.

Another who did not quite manage to reach the Hounslow starting line was Charles Kingsford Smith. Recently demobilized from the Royal Flying Corps, Lieutenant Kingsford Smith led a team including Cyril Brian Maddocks, Valdemar Rendle and (the South Australian) Leslie Booker. Their plan was to fly a Blackburn Kangaroo, but that proposal fell at the same hurdle as had Hinkler's earlier, since the Royal Aero Club insisted that none of the men had adequate navigational experience.[10] Kingsford Smith, who had fallen foul of the aricraft's manufacturer, licked his wounds and went on nearly a decade later to lead the first crew to fly across the Pacific.

Lieutenant W.H. Fysh – later Sir Hudson Fysh, one of the founders of Qantas – had hoped to compete in the race, but hopes were dashed by the sudden death of the wealthy pastoralist who had undertaken to bankroll the enterprise.[11]

The first valid entry was received from Val Rendle, who had been part of Kingsford Smith's proposed team but then became the chief pilot of a different crew with a Blackburn Kangaroo at their service. The captain of that crew was the prominent South Australian war photographer and explorer Hubert (later Sir Hubert) Wilkins, who persuaded the Royal Aero Club he had the wherewithal to navigate. With Rendle as main pilot, the other crew were David Reginald Williams and G.H.M. St Clair-Potts. Despite their early entry, a series of frustrating delays meant that they did not depart until 21 November, still full of hope that the prize would be theirs.

A month after Rendle and Wilkins, an entry was received from the Melbourne-born Raymond Parer and John McIntosh, who was Scottish-born but had moved to Australia before the war and had spent five gruelling months with the AIF at Gallipoli. Both men at the time held the rank of Lieutenant. Their plan was to fly an Airco

DH9, but any hope that they had of winning the race was cruelled by the difficulty of securing finance, with the result that they did not finally leave Hounslow until after the race was won.

After Bert Hinkler withdrew from the race, the Sopwith Aviation Company turned to Captain George Campbell Matthews of Adelaide and Sergeant Thomas D. Kay of Ballarat to fly their entry, a Sopwith Wallaby. Having donned Australian military khaki, Matthews and Kay were the first team to depart the official starting point, setting out to their first stop in Cologne in occupied Germany, where they received a cable from Billy Hughes, by now half a world away. 'If you cannot make Australia in 30 days, never mind,' he told them. 'The main thing is that an Australian should get here first.'[12]

The team of pilot Cedric Ernest Howell and navigator/mechanic George Henry Fraser flew a Martinsyde A1. Howell, born in Adelaide, had flown Sopwith Camels in Italy in the latter part of the war, while Fraser, the oldest man in the race, was an air mechanic attached to No 1 Bombing Squadron. Like most teams, their proposed route was through France, Italy and Greece, but as they were soon to find, the Mediterranean option was no guarantee of fine weather.

If bets were placed on the race, and no doubt they were, the smart money would have been on the team formed around Ross Smith. Smith had already flown as far east as Calcutta, and then he had surveyed much of the rest of the route by boat. Had the rules allowed it, Smith might have wished to fly again with Borton, but Borton was British and ineligible. In another way, however, Borton's influence was crucial, because he helped to secure for Smith a Vickers Vimy bomber. Intended to wreak havoc over German targets in the final phase of the war, the Vickers had since then proven its reliability on long-haul flights. In June 1919 the team of John W. Alcock and Arthur

Whitten Brown flew across the North Atlantic from Newfoundland to Ireland in 16 hours, winning a big prize offered by the *Daily Mail*. Heavy and cumbersome though the Vimy was, that triumph was a sign that it had the capacity and reliability to tackle the more daunting task of a flight across four continents and half a world.

Even so, for Ross Smith's purposes, and with the willing collaboration of the Vickers company, a number of changes were made to the Vimy to equip it for the race. A couple of Rolls-Royce Eagle VIII engines were fitted, gun mountings removed, the fuel storage increased, while the rear cockpit was fitted out to carry the two mechanics and spare parts.[13] Ross as pilot would share the front cockpit with his navigator. Emblazoned along the fuselage were the identification letters provided by the British Air Ministry: G-EAOU. The 'G' stood for Great Britain, but for its all-Australian crew, the letters were taken to stand for 'God 'Elp All of Us'.

View looking down on the Vickers Vimy, showing serial number 'G-EAOU' on top of the wings and on the side of the aircraft. [Ross and Keith Smith Collection, SLSA PRG 18/9/1/6A]

Keith Smith in the Royal Flying Corps, 1917.
[Ross and Keith Smith Collection, SLSA PRG 18/5/3]

With Borton ineligible, Ross brought into his crew as navigator his brother Keith, older than Ross by two years. Keith's early attempts to enlist in the AIF had failed twice for health reasons, but an operation enabled him finally to travel to the United Kingdom, where he was accepted by the Royal Flying Corps. Unlike Ross, for whom waging a war demanded almost daily acts of daring, Keith never saw action, devoting the largest part of his time to the instruction of pilots and navigators; his own flying was limited to northern England.[14] For the challenge that lay ahead, however, Keith was an ideal choice, having assembled a vast amount of theoretical and practical knowledge of navigation.

The mechanics Shiers and Bennett had both served in the Sinai and Palestine campaigns and flown with Ross Smith and Borton from Cairo to Calcutta; both had amassed experience in servicing aircraft and the engines on which the lives of all four depended. Born in Norwood to working class parents, Wally Shiers had worked for eight years in Broken Hill before the war. Like Ross Smith he had enlisted in the Light Horse but transferred to the No. 1 Squadron of the AFC, which is where he became acquainted with Ross. Jim Bennett, born in St Kilda, was the only non-South Australian in the Vimy.

There was one other entry among the official list of six, and that was by Roger Douglas and Leslie Ross. They had at their disposal a single-engined Alliance machine which they named *Endeavour* as a tribute to James Cook.

One other aircraft participated in the race, but not in an official capacity, and that was a French Caudron G-4, flown by Etienne Poulet in the company of his mechanic Jean Benoist. On a number of counts they were ineligible for the prize. To begin with, they were not Australians, and their plane was not of British

Left to right: Pilots Lieutenant Keith Smith and Captain Ross Smith,
with mechanics Sergeant James Bennett, and Sergeant Wally Shiers,
standing by the Vickers Vimy G-EAOU at Hounslow Heath, England,
at the start of the England to Australia flight. November 1919.
[Ross and Keith Smith Collection, SLSA PRG 18/9/1/3A]

manufacture. Moreover they commenced their flight from Paris, not from London as the race rules stipulated. In part Poulet was motivated by the memory of his late friend Jules Védrines, who had died when preparing an attempt to fly around the world.[15] Even if the Frenchmen would not be able to claim the prize, the glory of reaching Australia from Europe ahead of all the eligible teams beckoned. As Poulet was the first to embark on the epic flight, his tiny plane, ill-equipped for long distances and rough conditions, provided the hare for the Australian greyhounds to catch.

FLIGHT TO FAME

History shows that the Vickers Vimy won the air race, reaching Darwin on 10 December 1919, 28 days after departure from Hounslow, and after spending 135 hours in the air. It was one of just two teams to reach Darwin. On the day after the Vimy left London, the Alliance of Roger Douglas and Leslie Ross took to the skies, only to crash at Surbiton, a mere ten kilometres distant. Both men were dead within minutes of starting their race.

George Matthew and Thomas Kay had been the first team to leave London, but they made glacial progress in awful weather conditions, not reaching Vienna until 29 November. They limped on to Yugoslavia, a state in its troubled infancy. When forced down there they were set upon and arrested by armed men, then placed in detention with no hope of contacting the outside world. Eventually they managed to escape, reclaim their Wallaby and press on toward their goal. Reaching Constantinople a couple of days before Christmas, they learned that the race was already won, while they had still not cleared European air-space. They continued regardless, their flight dogged by mechanical failure and poor weather, as the

Wallaby hopped toward Darwin. Eventually, on 17 April, the Wallaby crashed in a banana plantation on Bali; Kay sustained broken ribs, and the plane was declared irreparable. The two men reached Sydney on 11 June, the remains of their Wallaby in their ship's hold.

Hubert Wilkins' Blackburn Kangaroo had been the fifth of the crews to depart Hounslow, nine days behind the Vickers Vimy, which by that time was somewhere over the Arabian desert. When they finally took off late in the morning of 21 November, Wilkins and his crew were waved off by Prince Albert, Winston Churchill and a couple of generals.[16] Plagued by mechanical problems, their bid reached its premature end in Crete. The Kangaroo had managed to take off from a sodden airfield at Suda Bay, surveyed the snow-capped peaks that formed the island's east-west spine and then set course for Cairo. Just as Wilkins was about to open a box of sandwiches, he was alerted to a catastrophic oil leak which forced the plane to return to Crete on just one engine. To prepare a landing, the pilot Val Rendle tried to restart the dead engine, but at once the water-jackets cracked and blew to pieces, sending fragments through the fuselage and sending the plane into a flat spin. It took all Rendle's skill to avoid crashing into the town of Canea. He pulled it up just in time for it to career across a field, drop into a ditch, burst all four tyres and then run straight at a solid wall. Fortunately a bank of earth stopped the Kangaroo just before the wall of a lunatic asylum, but its nose pitched forward, leaving its longing tail sticking into the air, signalling an ignominious yet at least injury-free end to the flight. As Wilkins later recalled, 'Somebody snickered, and in a moment we were all half paralysed with hysterical laughter.'[17] He abandoned hope of completing the race – which in any case the

Hubert Wilkins' Blackburn Kangaroo met an unfortunate end in Crete.

Smiths achieved as Wilkins' crew cooled their heels in Crete – and directed his spirit of adventure to the Antarctic.

Had there been a prize for persistence, it would surely have gone to 'battling' Ray Parer, who took a full seven months to complete the journey with John McIntosh. They flew a second-hand DH9, and did not leave London until the race was already over. As ill-fortune had already befallen or was to befall almost all of the others, they became just the second crew to make their destination.

As for the French team of Etienne Poulet and his mechanic Jean Benoist, flying for national pride rather than Billy Hughes's prize, their Caudron was eventually reeled in by the Vimy at Akyab (today's Sittwe) in Burma. Damage to one of the Caudon's propellers meant Poulet had to abandon his dream of reaching Australia on 9 December – the day before the Vimy reached Darwin.

While history records the triumph of the Vimy, Ross Smith's account of the flight reveals just how many challenges and hazards the crew faced along the way. The cold endured between London and Lyons prompted him to record in his diary, 'This sort of flying

The French team of Etienne Poulet and Jean Benoist in front of their
Caudron G-4 on the eve of their departure in the race. [Air Journal, France]

is a rotten game. The cold is hell and I am a silly ass for having
ever embarked on the flight.'[18] At Pisa the Vimy had sunk so far
into a sodden airfield that it barely managed to get off the ground.
At Allahabad (now officially known as Prayagraj) a large bull broke
into the aerodrome just as the Vimy was preparing to take off; it
pawed the ground as if threatening to charge the aircraft. When
departing Calcutta (Kolkata), two hawks flew straight at the plane,
one smashing into a wing, the other into the port propeller, which
thankfully withstood the impact and helped haul the Vimy over
the trees bordering the racecourse. The racecourse serving as an
airfield in Rangoon – today's Yangon – was so short that Smith
barely gathered enough speed to take off, the Vimy's undercarriage
brushing tree tops on the way. In landing in Singora Smith had
to negotiate a recently-cleared runway covered with tree stumps,
while at Surabaya in the Dutch East Indies the Vimy was bogged and
had to take off from an improvised airstrip made of bamboo mats,
provided at short notice by locals.

What Smith's modesty prevented him from conveying fully in his book was the enthusiasm of the reception he and his crew received in Australia. As the Vimy winged its way from Timor to Darwin, excited word spread of its impending arrival, and crowds gathered at the Fanny Bay aerodrome. Among those present when the Vimy touched down at 3.40 on the afternoon of 10 December was the local quarantine officer, who in examining all four airmen commenced a tradition with which air-travellers to Australia have become all too familiar in the century since then. The official, a certain Dr Harris, had to restrain a woman who rushed forward the moment the Vimy landed, warning her of the risk of catching a terrible disease. She replied, 'I will take that chance to be the first to shake the hand of Ross Smith.'[19]

Though the prize was won with the arrival in Darwin, and the Vimy the worse for wear after the rigours of nearly a month's flight, the crew was keen to continue south. At every point between Darwin and Adelaide there was a rapturous welcome. There was also frustration. Eager not to sully in any way the reputation of the Vimy, Ross Smith says little of the mechanical troubles that plagued the aircraft between Darwin and its final destination. On Christmas Day of 1919, and just outside Charleville in Queensland, there was a terrific bang aboard the aircraft. A flash of fire shot from one of the engines, and Ross had to fight with the controls to perform an emergency landing. A split in the propeller had broken a piston rod, causing what might have otherwise been a disastrous failure. At first it was feared this might be the end of the flight, but a plan was hatched to repair the engine in Ipswich. Not until 12 February – some 50 days later – could the journey continue. Over three days, with stops in Bourke and Narromine, Ross nursed the Vimy to Sydney and then on to Melbourne, where the airman gratefully accepted their reward from Billy Hughes. The £10,000 prize was shared evenly among the four airmen, since all in Ross's view had shared evenly in the 'perils and labours of the enterprise'.[20]

The silver lining in the cloud of the Queensland lay-up was the opportunity for Ross Smith to renew his acquaintance with Frank Hurley, who in the meantime had returned to Australia from his own wartime duties. Almost inseparable from his camera, Hurley took a series of photographs and film of the final legs of the epic flight; many of the photos found their way into his friend Ross Smith's book, offering its readers a new perspective on a country hauling itself from the trauma of war and looking to the future.

Had Vickers had its way, the flight would have terminated in Melbourne, the handing over of the cheque a fitting conclusion. But Ross disregarded Vickers' wishes and chose to continue on to Adelaide, his home town. It was a decision supported by both the South Australian government and by Billy Hughes, conscious that to complete a flight from Melbourne to Adelaide would be yet another first.

When the Vimy passed over the Adelaide GPO at 1.55 pm on 23 March 1920, cannons were fired and crowds cheered. Ross brought the Vimy down low enough to wave to all those gathered at the Enfield aerodrome of Harry J. Butler and Kauper Company. The plane landed to the acclaim of thronging South Australians in fields besides the North East Road. They were there to welcome and ogle at a machine unlike any they had seen before. More than that, they were to stage a homecoming worthy of three of their own who had survived the most remarkable flight in history. Since leaving London the men had spent a total of 188 hours and 20 minutes in the air and had covered a distance of 23,090 kilometres.

Aerial view of Adelaide taken from on board the Vickers Vimy,
showing Ross Smith flying the aircraft into Adelaide, 23 March 1920.
[Ross and Keith Smith Collection, SLSA PRG 18/7/75]

The fame earned by Ross Smith and those who flew with him was well recognised at the time. Both he and brother Keith were knighted as early as 22 December 1919, within a couple of weeks of their arrival in Darwin. Bennett and Shiers received Bars to their Air Force Medals and were commissioned.

Such was the demand to hear from Ross Smith the insider's version of the epic flight that he toured widely, addressing enthusiastic crowds. For the first time in years, flying took a back seat. An insatiable public lapped up lengthy accounts he wrote for *National Geographic* and *Life*. Frank Hurley used the footage he had taken to make a documentary movie titled *The Ross Smith Flight*. It was first presented at a vice-regal night at the Sydney Town Hall and then went on tour of Australia and the UK for several months.[21]

As he generously acknowledges on his book's very first page, Ross relied heavily on the advice and enthusiasm of Frank Hurley in putting together a book about the flight, drawing not only on his own fresh memories but on images and ideas with which Hurley plied him. Keith, too, provided invaluable input, not only because he had kept a faithful logbook, but because he had made use of a camera of the kind which the Kodak Company had made available to all the entrants in the race. Where Hurley's photographs documented the final, Australian legs of the flight, Keith's Kodak provided a visual record of the adventures and travails between London and Darwin.

Just as the book was about to be published to quench the thirst of an insatiable public, Ross returned to flying. The plan he hatched with Keith was to become the first to fly around the world. Vickers would once more provide them with the mechanical means to realise their dream. This time it was to be an amphibious aircraft, a Vickers Viking.

On 13 April 1922, in preparation for that next great challenge, Ross was to test fly the Viking, an aircraft with which he was unfamiliar. He did so at the Vickers works near London. With him on that day was Jim Bennett. Keith Smith was to join them for that flight but was running late and missed it. Just minutes after take-off the aircraft fell from the sky, spinning wildly out of control. Both Smith and Bennett were killed.

Even in peacetime, violent death was part of the reality which the pioneers of aviation accepted with equanimity. Such were the hazards of early flight that one of Vickers' early test pilots, Stan Cockerell, once commented that the first duty of every aviator was to learn to crash.[22] Ross Smith and Jim Bennett died in the service of aviation within three years of the race's conclusion, while John McIntosh of the DH9 was killed in a plane crash in Western Australia in March 1921. In a cruel irony, the mortality rate among this elite group in peacetime was much higher than in the AIF at war. Moreover, tragedy continued to stalk their former comrades in arms in the years that followed. Bert Hinkler met his death crossing the Italian Alps in 1933. Kingsford Smith came to grief flying the *Lady Southern Cross* over the Andaman Sea two years later. Charles Ulm, who like Ross Smith had served at Gallipoli, and who reached the apex of his fame when crossing the Pacific with Kingsford Smith, disappeared over that same ocean in 1934.

Among all these men, fame extracted a heavy price, yet it lives on. Their courage and endurance, legendary even in their own short lives, have produced an enduring afterlife and given wings to the imaginations of all who have followed in their slipstreams.

NOTES

1   This and other wartime letters by Ross Smith to his mother Jessie Smith are held in the State Library of South Australia, SLSA PRG 18/17.

2   SLSA PRG 18/17.

3   Nelson Eustis, *The Greatest Air Race: England – Australia 1919*, Adelaide: Rigby, 1969, 110.

4   A. Grenfell Price, *The Skies Remember: The Story of Ross and Keith Smith*, Sydney: Angus & Robertson, 1969, 57.

5   T.E. Lawrence, *The Seven Pillars of Wisdom*, New York: Open Road, 2015, 485.

6   Price, *The Skies Remember*, 61.

7   Frank Hurley, 'The Great War Diary', 16 February 1918. In Robert Dixon and Christopher Lee (eds), *The Diaries of Frank Hurley 1912–1941*, London: Anthem, 2011, 96–97.

8   Cited in Eustis, *The Greatest Air Race*, 2.

9   Simon Nasht, *The Last Explorer: Hubert Wilkins, Australia's Unknown Hero*, Sydney: Hodder, 2005, 80.

10 Eustis, *The Greatest Air Race*, 16.

11 Eustis, *The Greatest Air Race*, 19.

12 Cited in Eustis, *The Greatest Air Race*, 41.

13 Price, *The Skies Remember*, 82.

14 Price, *The Skies Remember*, 129.

15 Nasht, *The Last Explorer*, 84.

16 Lowell Thomas, *Sir Hubert Wilkins: His World of Adventure*, London: Arthur Barker, 1962, 111.

17 Thomas, *Sir Hubert Wilkins*, 115.

18 Price, *The Skies Remember*, 90–91.

19 Cited in Eustis, *The Greatest Air Race*, 152.

20 Price, *The Skies Remember*, 114.

21 Frank Legg, *Once More on My Adventure*, Sydney: Ure Smith, 1966, 112.

22 Cited in Price, *The Skies Remember*, 118.

A NOTE ON THE TEXT

Ross Smith's account of the record-breaking Vickers Vimy flight from England to Australia was first published in 1922 by Macmillan under the title *14,000 Miles Through the Air: The First Flight from England to Australia*. Ross Smith records finishing the writing of the manuscript in September 1921, some eighteen months after his arrival in Adelaide. Earlier, briefer narratives had been published in the American *National Geographic Magazine* and in Australian *Life*.

Without a doubt Frank Hurley made a significant contribution to the writing of the book, not least by suggesting the idea to Ross Smith in the first place. Indeed Ross Smith explicitly acknowledges Hurley's 'generous and energetic help'. The two men knew each other from the time when Hurley was a war photographer and Smith a pilot in the Australian Flying Corps. Hurley joined the Vimy for the final stages of its flight from Charleville in Queensland.

This edition is faithful to the original Macmillan edition of 1922, with a new title and minor orthographic and formatting adjustments. In the century since the Vimy's flight, the world has changed immensely. Above all it is less British than it was then, so footnotes have been added above all to aid the reader in relating the geopolitics of 1919 to the present.

Captain Frank Hurley and Keith Smith on the Vickers Vimy at Charleville, Queensland. [Ross and Keith Smith Collection, SLSA PRG 18/55/3]

The 1922 edition of the book contained numerous photographs by Hurley, which did much to convey to the reader the Australian portions of the flight. As for the rest, fortunately the crew members had available to them a camera and dozens of films provided by the Kodak company. They were used to great effect by Keith Smith, Jim Bennett and Wally Shiers, who managed to win the prize of £800 offered by Kodak for the best 50 negatives. Some of those photographs featured in the original edition alongside Hurley's work, while for this new edition a fresh selection of images has been made. It draws on the rich collection of material relating to the Vimy's flight held in the State Library of South Australia.

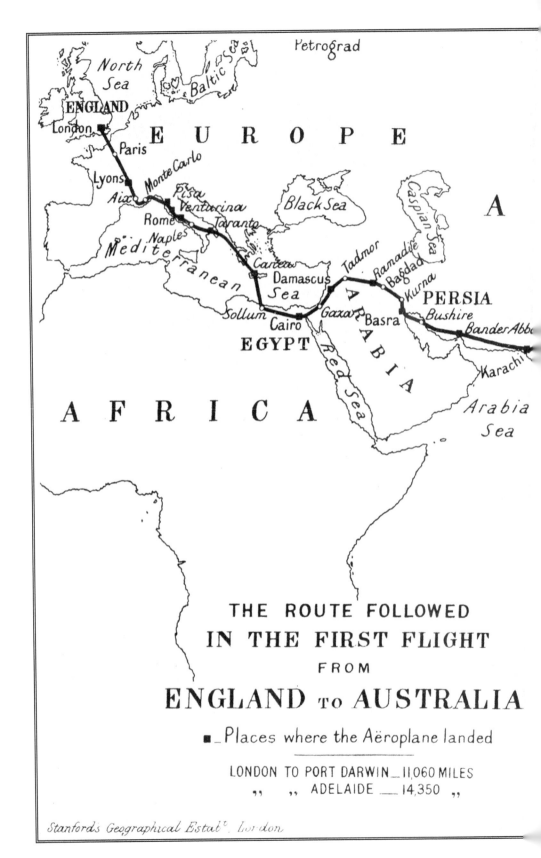

THE ROUTE FOLLOWED
IN THE FIRST FLIGHT
FROM
ENGLAND TO AUSTRALIA

■ _ Places where the Aëroplane landed

LONDON TO PORT DARWIN _ 11,060 MILES
,,   ,,   ADELAIDE _ 14,350 ,,

Stanford's Geographical Estab?. London

S I A
Peking
CHINA
JAPAN
Tokyo
Delhi
Muttra
Allahabad
Calcutta
Chittagong
DIA
Akyab
mbay
Moulmein
SIAM
Rangoon
Bangkok
Pacific
Philippine Is.
Ocean
Ceylon
Singora
Singapore
Muntok
Batavia
Soerabaya
Bima
Atamboea
DUTCH EAST INDIES
Kalidjati
Port Darwin
Indian
Warlock Ponds
Anthony's Lagoon
Cloncurry
Ocean
AUSTRALIA
Charleville
Bourke
Cootamundra
Henty
Adelaide
Sydney
Melbourne
Tasmania

TIME TABLE WITH DISTANCE

Date	Hour	Route	Time in Air (hours mins.)	Distance (miles)
12/11/1919	09.05	London to Lyons	6 20	500
13/11/1919	10.06	Lyons to Pisa	4 45	380
15/11/1919	10.00	Pisa to Rome	3 20	180
16/11/1919	09.04	Rome to Taranto	2 35	260
17/11/1919	08.15	Taranto to Suda Bay (Crete)	5 40	520
18/11/1919	08.12	Suda Bay to Cairo	7 20	650
19/11/1919	10.24	Cairo to Damascus	4 10	450
20/11/1919	10.15	Damascus to Ramadie	6 00	420
21/11/1919	13.15	Ramadie to Basra	3 30	350
23/11/1919	06.35	Basra to Bundar Abbas	7 40	630
24/11/1919	07.00	Bundar Abbas to Karachi	8 30	730
25/11/1919	07.40	Karachi to Delhi	9 00	720
27/1/1919	10.20	Delhi to Allahabad	4 25	380
28/11/1919	08.30	Allahabad to Calcutta	5 00	470
29/11/1919	08.30	Calcutta to Akyab (Burma)	4 45	420
30/11/1919	07.30	Akyab to Rangoon	4 15	330
1/12/1919	06.55	Rangoon to Bangkok	6 00	400
2/12/1919	07.45	Bangkok to Singora	6 00	470
4/12/1919	10.15	Singora to Singapore	6 20	480
6/12/1919	07.00	Singapore to Kalidjati (Java)	9 00	640
7/12/1919	07.35	Kalidjati to Surabaya	4 20	350
8/12/1919	12.00	Surabaya to Bima (Sumbawa)	5 00	420
9/12/1919	09.45	Bima to Atamboea (Timor)	5 30	440
10/12/1919	08.35	Atamboea to Port Darwin (Australia)	6 30	470
13/12/1919	10.23	Port Darwin to Warlock Ponds	4 20	220
14/12/1919	09.00	Warlock Ponds to Cobb's Creek	5 30	300
17/12/1919	18.00	Cobb's Creek to Anthony's Lagoon	0 15	20
18/12/1919	10.05	Anthony's Lagoon to Brunette Downs	1 00	50
19/12/1919	11.05	Brunette Downs to Avon Downs	2 45	180
20/12/1919	07.45	Avon Downs to Cloncurry	3 00	230
22/12/1919	06.50	Cloncurry to Longreach	4 40	300
23/12/1919	07.05	Longreach to Charleville	3 40	330
12/2/1920	11.00	Charleville to Bourke	4 00	260
13/2/1920	09.00	Bourke to Narromine	3 00	230
14/2/1920	07.00	Narromine to Sydney	4 15	200
23/2/1920	10.05	Sydney to Cootamundra	4 15	240
24/2/1920	10.00	Cootamundra to Henty	1 10	80
25/2/1920	06.00	Henty to Melbourne	3 05	220
23/3/1920	07.00	Melbourne to Adelaide	7 30	430
		Total flying time and distance, London to Adelaide	**188 20**	**14,350**

In addition to the above, several hours were spent in the air making test flights at various places.

Preface

My thanks are due to Captain Frank Hurley for his generous and energetic help in the writing of this book. Had it not been for his persuasion and hard work, I doubt if it even would have been accomplished. When it was first suggested to me that I should write an account of the Vimy's flight from England to Australia, I thought it a splendid idea and at once said that I would. That was 15 months ago and I have only just completed it! I have tried to tell the story just as I remember it and without too much technical detail and in doing this my brother's diary has been of the greatest assistance.

A slightly shorter account of this flight first appeared in the Washington *National Geographic Magazine* and in Australian *Life* and I am indebted to these publications for their courtesy in allowing me to reproduce it.

Ross Smith
London, September, 1921

Ross Smith with General Borton in the Handley Page on the Cairo–Calcutta flight, December 1918. [Ross and Keith Smith Collection, SLSA PRG 18/6/1]

CHAPTER I

Preparations

During the latter phase of the war, while I was flying with Number One Squadron, Australian Flying Corps, in Palestine, a Handley-Page aeroplane was flown out from England by Brigadier-General A.E. Borton, CMG, DSO, AFC, to take part in General Allenby's last offensive. It was intended that this monster aeroplane should be chiefly employed in carrying out active night-bombing operations against the enemy. I hailed as good fortune the orders that detailed me to fly it. The remarkable success eventually achieved by this terrible engine of destruction, and its unfailing reliability during the ensuing long-distance flights, inspired in me great confidence and opened my eyes to the possibilities of modern aeroplanes and their application to commercial uses.

It is in a large measure due to the extensive experiences gained while piloting this Handley-Page machine that I was induced to embark upon and carry to a successful issue the first aerial voyage from London to Australia. In a lesser degree, the undertaking was suggested in a joke. One day General Borton visited our squadron and informed me that he was planning a flight in order to link up the forces in Palestine with the army in Mesopotamia. He invited me to join him.

There was a further proposal, that after reaching Bagdad we should shape a route to India, 'to see,' as he jocularly remarked, 'the Viceroy's Cup run in Calcutta.'[1]

'Then, after that', I replied, 'let us fly on to Australia and see the Melbourne Cup', little thinking at the time that I should ever embark upon such a project.

Just after the Armistice was signed, General Borton decided to start out in the Handley-Page for India. Major-General Sir W.G.H. Salmond, KCMG, CB, DSO, commanding the Royal Air Force in the Middle East, would accompany us and carry out a tour of inspection.

On November 29, 1918, we took our departure from Cairo, accompanied by my two air mechanics, Sergeant J.M. Bennett, AFM, MSM, and Sergeant W.H. Shiers, AFM, both of Number One Squadron. It took just three weeks to pioneer a route to India, where we arrived, without mishap, on December 10, 1918, scarcely a month after the signing of the Armistice.

Major-General Salmond was very proud of this achievement, for it demonstrated that the new arm of the service, the Royal Air Force, had begun to concentrate its efforts on peaceful developments and the establishment of long-distance commercial air routes.

This was the longest flight that had ever been made up to this time, and it convinced me that a machine, properly attended and equipped, was capable of flying anywhere, provided suitable landing grounds existed.

After our arrival in India, General Borton communicated with the Air Ministry and asked for permission to charter a steamer to enable him to proceed to Australia to explore the route and arrange suitable landing grounds.

---

1   Kolkata

I was to accompany General Borton on this expedition as his staff captain, and it was our intention, after surveying out the route, to return to India, join up with our machine, which we had left at Lahore, and continue the flight to Australia over the established course.

The Air Ministry acceded to General Borton's wishes, and the Indian Government accordingly placed at our disposal the RIMS *Sphinx*. On February 10, 1919, we sailed from Calcutta, our hold stowed tight with stores and equipment and 7,000 gallons of petrol. We intended to dump 200 gallons of petrol at each landing place for the anticipated flight. But all our well-laid schemes ended in smoke.

Two days later, just after leaving Chittagong, in East Bengal, our first port of call, the *Sphinx* caught fire and blew up. We narrowly escaped going up with it. We lost everything but our lives. After this mishap we were compelled to return to India to refit. The Indian Government generously lent us another vessel, the RIMS *Minto*. This time we carried no petrol. The expedition was rewarded with splendid success during the period of three months we were engaged upon it. We visited Burma, the Federated Malay States, the Netherlands Indies, Borneo, and Siam.

Upon our return to India we were chagrined to find that our machine had been taken up to the Northwest Frontier to participate in a bombing offensive against the Afghans, and had been crashed in a storm.

However, our heart-pangs were mitigated when we learned that the Australian Commonwealth Government had offered a prize of £10,000 for the first machine (manned by Australians) to fly from London to Australia in 30 days.

Hearing this, I knew there would be many competitors, and the spirit of rivalry grew tense. It stimulated in me a keenness—more than ever—to attempt the flight. My difficulty was how to reach England in time.

Shortly afterward General Borton was instructed to return to London to report on the route. This opened the avenue of transport for myself and my two mechanics. General Borton himself was very keen to join in the flight to Australia, but, unfortunately, not being an Australian he was debarred from entering the competition. He very kindly approached Messrs Vickers Ltd, and asked them if they would supply a machine for the flight. This, at first, they refused to do, but after General Borton pointed out that I had already done a considerable amount of long-distance flying and had been over nearly the whole route, as well as assisted in pioneering it, they finally consented.

My brother Keith was at the time in England waiting repatriation to Australia. During the latter part of the war he had been flying with the Royal Air Force and had gained extensive and varied air experience. I therefore decided that he would be the best man to take as assistant pilot and navigator.

Sergeants Bennett and Shiers, in view of their excellent war services and the knowledge that they gained in the flight from Cairo to Calcutta, were to accompany us as air mechanics, thus making a total crew of four.

Vickers did not definitely decide to enter the machine for the competition until October, and as we left London on November 12th, it will be seen that the time to prepare for such an undertaking was very limited. Our preparations were doubly hurried, first by the knowledge that four other machines had entered the competition and were actually ready to start before the Vickers Company had handed over their machine to us, and, second, by the fact that winter was fast approaching and the season might break at any time, thus rendering long-distance flying extremely unpleasant.

Once Vickers had decided to enter the machine, however, they threw themselves whole-heartedly into the project and practically gave me a free hand to make whatever arrangements I deemed essential. I had gone minutely into all the intricate details of equipment, the question of supplies, fuel, etc., during my return voyage to England.

The 'Shell' Marketing Co. agreed to have our petrol supplies at the required depôts to tabulated dates, and Messrs Wakefield Ltd, in a similar capacity undertook to arrange for lubricating oils. The route I decided upon was, roughly, England, France, Italy, Crete, Egypt, Palestine, Mesopotamia, Persia, India, Burma, Siam, Federated Malay States, Dutch East Indies to Port Darwin.

With the route from Port Darwin to our ultimate destination we were unconcerned, for we had received intimation that the Defence Department of Australia had made all necessary arrangements. The great thing was to reach Australia, and, if possible, land our machine there under thirty days.

For my convenience, I divided the route into four stages: First, London to Cairo; second, Cairo to Calcutta; third, Calcutta to Singapore; fourth, Singapore to Australia.

I had been over the entire route with the exception of the first stage, and so was fairly cognizant of the existing conditions—the weather, climate, and the nature of the landing grounds. General Borton had pioneered the first stage in August, 1918; his generous advice, directions, charts, and photographs were invaluable.

For the first two stages bad weather was my only apprehension.

As far as Calcutta, passable aerodromes existed, and I could rest assured of Royal Air Force assistance at almost every landing place.

From Calcutta onward we would be entirely dependent on our own arrangements. I considered these last two stages the most hazardous of the flight. Owing to the dense jungles and rough ground, landing places were few and far between, and even those at which we contemplated stopping were very small and unsuited to landing a big machine.

After leaving Calcutta, I proposed landing on the race-course at Rangoon,[2] from which I would fly across the mountain ranges to the Siamese aerodrome at Bangkok. I then proposed to skirt southward down the coast of the Malay Peninsula to Singapore, where once more a landing would be made on a race-course.

The next stop would be made at the hangars of the Dutch Flying School, near Batavia.[3] There would then be no further aerodromes until Port Darwin was reached, a distance of 1,750 miles. I knew that the Vickers Vimy was quite capable of carrying out a non-stop flight of that distance, for this had been demonstrated by the late Captain Sir John Alcock, KBE, DSC, on his famous transatlantic flight; but I was also aware that to attempt such a long flight with engines that by that time would have done over 100 hours' running and covered nearly 10,000 miles would be too much to expect.

I therefore decided that, in order to make more nearly certain my chances of success, an aerodrome must be constructed midway. General Borton had selected an admirable site at Bima,[4] on the island of Sumbawa, in the Dutch East Indies. If a

---

2   Yangon

3   Jakarta

4   The Sultanate of Bima was a Muslim state under indirect Dutch rule.

landing could be made there, the long stage of 1,750 miles would be halved and the possibility of success more than doubled.

When on my previous visit to Java, I had had the honour of a lengthy interview with His Excellency the Governor-General, Count Van Limburg Stirum[5], concerning the aerodromes which General Borton and I were selecting in the Netherlands Indies for the proposed aerial route to Australia. His Excellency was most enthusiastic over the development of commercial aviation, and I found him particularly well informed on all aerial matters. He also stated that any aerial route passing over the Netherlands Indies would receive his whole-hearted support and the assistance of his government.

In the course of the conversation I mentioned that I hoped, personally, to attempt the flight from England to Australia a few months later. He said that he would be gratified to assist in any capacity. Remembering this while in London, I decided to ask His Excellency if he would prepare an aerodrome at the selected site at Bima, and sent off a private cable.

Ten valuable days elapsed before I received a reply, but when it came I was overjoyed to learn that he was not only having Bima prepared, but also another aerodrome at Atamboea[6], in the island of Timor. This greatly eased my mind, for it meant that instead of having to accommodate our machine with a petrol capacity for 1,750 miles, we need only install tanks for a non-stop flight of 1,000 miles. This greatly added to the buoyancy of the machine, and, through the saving in space, to our personal comfort.

---

5   Johan Paul van Limburg Stirum was Governor-General of the Dutch East Indies from 1916 to 1921.

6   Atambua

The machine was an ordinary Standard Vickers Vimy bomber, similar to that used by Sir John Alcock for the transatlantic flight, and, apart from the installing of an extra petrol tank, we made practically no alterations.

The machine was powered by two Rolls-Royce Eagle VIII engines, each of 360 horse-power. The wing-spread was a little over 67 feet and the total weight, loaded, was six and a half tons.

Vickers' factory, the home of the Vimy, is at Weybridge, about 20 miles distant from London, and is built by the side of the famous Brooklands motor-racing track. After completing the office work in London, the four of us moved to Weybridge and practically lived on the machine.

The fitting, testing, and final adjusting were thoroughly interesting, and great enthusiasm was shown by the employees of Vickers. It was gratifying to observe that these same men and women, who had produced the great machine flown by Sir John Alcock, felt that their efforts were something more than mere labour. They were producing an ideal from their factory to uphold national prestige. Every man and woman did his or her best, and wished us God-speed.

Thus we were able to place the deepest confidence in the machine; we feared no frailties in its manufacture, and hundreds of times during the flight we had occasion to pay tribute to and praise the sterling efforts of those British workers.

Our petrol capacity would carry us for 13 hours at a cruising speed of 80 miles an hour—ample for the longest stages between aerodromes.

The question of 'spares' was of vital importance and one into which I had previously gone minutely. As we intended starting almost immediately, I decided that it would be useless to ship 'spares' ahead, so that the only course left was to carry them with us. This added considerably to the weight of the machine; but the absence of a certain spare part, should we require it, might delay us for weeks, and so put us out of the competition.

Eventually the spare parts, personal kit, and miscellaneous gear were assembled and weighed. I decided to limit the total weight of our machine when fully loaded to 13,000 pounds.

I was aware that the deadweight of Sir John Alcock's machine in the transatlantic flight was over 14,000 pounds, but in the vastly greater distance that lay before us, I intended to give my engines as little work as possible.

We discovered that, after the 'weighing in', there was an excess of 300 pounds; so something had to go. Our 'spares' were indispensable, and so we drastically attacked our personal kit. It was easy enough to cut down our kit—so soon as we were unanimous in deciding to go without any- and so it eventuated that we left England in the garments we wore and with the proverbial toothbrush apiece.

As my brother was navigator, all arrangements concerning maps, etc., were left entirely to him. Wherever possible, we would fly our course by maps and direct observations of features on the ground; but when cloudy or misty weather rendered terrestrial observation obscure, we would rely solely on navigation. For this purpose we carried an Admiralty compass, a ground-speed and drift indicator, and we had our own flying experience to fall back on.

We discussed the question of carrying a wireless set at some length and finally decided not to take one. It would weigh 100 pounds and take up a good deal of room and would be of little use to us except for sending cheery messages to various places we passed over.

Mechanics Walter Shiers and James Bennett assessing the engine and propeller of the Vickers Vimy, c. 1919. [Ross and Keith Smith Collection, SLSA PRG 18/8/7]

These days of preparation at Weybridge passed very rapidly. Bennett and Shiers worked on the Vimy helping to put the finishing touches to her, while Keith and I busied ourselves with the hundred and one details that such an expedition entails.

Previously I had been from England to Australia several times by mail steamer and on each occasion I had embarked either at Tilbury or Marseilles and in due course reached Adelaide and thought very little about the journey. But here was something vastly different.

This time we had an aeroplane at Brooklands aerodrome and somewhere away on the other side of the world was Australia. We were going to climb up into the air and *fly* through thousands of miles of space to our own home! It was to be a great adventure— this skimming through 'unflown skies', over strange lands, and vast spaces of ocean. Furthermore, we were attempting something which had never before been done, and so it is no wonder that we were elated at the prospect and went about our work with eagerness and light hearts.

I knew that the physical and nervous strain of long flying hours day after day would be great, so we all went into training and generally took care of ourselves. At night we would work on the maps, plotting out the course and studying the prominent landmarks, and so long before we left England we had practically visualised most of the country that we were to fly over.

For food we carried an emergency ration consisting of tinned meat and biscuits, together with some chocolate and Bovril. This was in case we should be forced to land in some obscure place and, roughly, we had enough food to last us seven days. However, ordinarily we contemplated getting sufficient food to last us for the next day at each place at which we landed. A fishing line and a few hooks were also

carried in case we should land on some small uninhabited island and have to do the 'Robinson Crusoe' act for a time.

As we were to fly over several foreign countries, the International Air Convention required that we should have a distinctive number or mark painted on the machine in the same manner as a motor car has to carry a number plate. The Air Ministry allotted us the letters 'G–E A O U', which were painted on the wings and fuselage, the 'G'

The Vickers Vimy, on a snowy day at Hounslow, London 12/11/1919.
In flying clothes, from left to right: Ross Smith, Keith Smith,
Sergeant Bennett and Sergeant Shiers. The tall man between
and Shiers is R.K. Pierson, the designer of the Vickers Vimy.
[Ross and Keith Smith Collection, SLSA PRG 18/9/1/9A]

standing for Great Britain and 'E A O U' representing our number.
However, in view of the long flight which we contemplated, our own
interpretation of this marking was 'God 'Elp All Of Us'!

The machine was at last ready, and, after being flown and tested by Sir John Alcock, was pronounced fit for the undertaking. I considered it advisable to remain another week in England in order to give our supplies of fuel and oil sufficient time to reach some of the more remote aerodromes.

It was galling to have to idle in England while every day we read in the press of the progress of Monsieur Poulet, who had left Paris on October 14th and had by now reached Mesopotamia. The Sopwith machine, piloted by Captain Matthews, had also left England some time previously.

The weather during this week's stay was abominable. Winter was fast closing in with typical English November fogs. Driving sleet and pelting rains fell almost without intermission. One afternoon there was a brief lull, and I managed to get the machine into the air for about an hour and make a final test.

Our machine was still at Weybridge, and the official starting place for the competitive flight was the Hounslow aerodrome.

I had intended flying over to Hounslow on November 13th and starting off on the flight the following morning. On November 11th we were pottering around our machine when the rain suddenly ceased and the fog lifted. It was too good an opportunity to miss! We ran the machine out of its hangar, and I was just about to start up when the clouds closed down again and snow fell heavily.

The weather was very capricious, for in half an hour the clouds rolled away, clearing the air and giving promise of a bright, fine evening. The engines were started up, we climbed into our seats, and took off from Weybridge. As far as we were concerned, the flight to Australia had begun!

During the voyage to Hounslow the machine in every part worked to my entire satisfaction and we landed at the official starting ground without difficulty.

Hounslow was then the main 'civilian' aerodrome of London and all commercial machines inward and outward bound from or to the Continent started from or landed there. So soon as the machine was in its hangar, I got in touch with Vickers and informed them that I intended starting next morning.

On the morning of November 12th we were called at 4.30 and I was delighted to find a clear, frosty morning. However, at 6.30 a dense ground haze appeared, and weather reports sent by the Air Ministry forecasted bad weather in the southeast of England and the north of France.

The machine was run out from the hangars and Commander Perrin, of the Royal Aero Club, marked and sealed five parts of it, in accordance with the rules of the competition. It was necessary to produce three of the marked parts upon arrival in Australia, in order to identify the machine.

At 8 o'clock another report stated that the forecast was Class V, or totally unfit for flying. This was not very reassuring, but our minds were made up and, come fair, come foul, we were determined to start.

A few friends had gathered to bid us God-speed, and, with their kindly expressions and cheers sounding in our ears, we climbed into our seats and took off from the snow-covered aerodrome.

CHAPTER II

Through Cloud Ocean to Lyons

We climbed slowly upward through the cheerless, mist-laden skies, our engines well throttled back and running perfectly. So as to make sure that all was in thorough working order, we circled for ten minutes above Hounslow, then set off.

At 2,000 feet we suddenly emerged from the fog belt into brilliant sunshine, but the world below was lost to sight, screened by the dense pall of mist. Accordingly, we set a compass course for Folkestone, and just before reaching the outskirts a rift in the mists enabled us to pick up the grand old coast-line, every inch of which is measured by history; and so we checked our bearings.

There was a certain amount of sentiment, mingled with regrets, in leaving old England, the land of our fathers. Stormy seas were sweeping up channel, lashing white foam against the gaunt, grey cliffs that peered through the mists in the winter light, phantom-like and unreal.

The frigid breath of winter stung our faces and chilled us through; its garb of white had fallen across the land, making the prospect inexpressibly drear. The roadways, etched in dark relief, stood out like pencil-lines on the snow-clad landscape, all converging on Folkestone.

I looked over the side as the town itself, which had played such an important part in the war, came under us. Thither the legions of the Empire, in ceaseless tides, had passed to and from the grim red fields of East and West, all acclaiming thy might, great land of our fathers!

It seemed hard to realise that we had at last started out on the long flight for which we had been planning and working so long, and as I glanced over the machine and the instruments, I wondered what the issue of it all might be—if the fates would be so kind as to smile on us ever so little and allow us to reach the goal of our ambitions, Australia, in thirty days.

The machine was flying stately and steady as a rock. All the bracing wires were tuned to a nicety; the dope on the huge planes glinted and glistened in the sunlight; I was filled with admiration. The engines, which were throttled down to about three-quarters of their possible speed, had settled down to their task and were purring away in perfect unison and harmony.

A small machine is ideal for short flights, joy-riding the heavens, or sight-seeing among the clouds; but there is something more majestic and stable about the big bombers which a pilot begins to love. An exquisite community grows up between machine and pilot; each, as it were, merges into the other. The machine is rudimentary and the pilot the intellectual force. The levers and controls are the nervous system of the machine, through which the will of the pilot may be expressed—and expressed to an infinitely fine degree. A flying machine is something entirely apart from and above all other contrivances of man's ingenuity.

The aeroplane is the nearest thing to animate life that man has created. In the air a machine ceases indeed to be a mere piece of mechanism; it becomes animate and is capable not only of primary guidance and control, but actually of expressing a pilot's temperament.

The lungs of the machine, its engines, are again the crux of man's wisdom. Their marvellous reliability and great intricacy are almost as awesome as the human anatomy. When both engines are going well and synchronized to the same speed, the roar of the exhausts develops into one long-sustained rhythmical boom-boom-boom. It is a song of pleasant harmony to the pilot, a duet of contentment that sings of perfect firing in both engines and says that all is well.

This melody of power boomed pleasantly in my ears, and my mind sought to probe the inscrutable future, as we swept over the coast of England at 90 miles per hour.

And then the sun came out brightly and the Channel, all flecked with white tops, spread beneath us. Two torpedo-boats, looking like toys, went northward. And now, midway, how narrow and constricted the Straits appeared, with the grey-white cliffs of old England growing misty behind, and ahead—Gris Nez—France, growing detail each moment!

The weather was glorious, and I was beginning to think that the official prophet, who had predicted bad conditions at our start, was fallible after all. It was not until we reached the coast of France that the oracle justified itself; for, stretching away as far as we could see, there lay a sea of cloud. Thinking it might be only a local belt, we plunged into the compacted margin, only to discover a dense wall of nimbus cloud, heavily surcharged with snow.

The machine speedily became deluged by sleet and snow. It clotted up our goggles and the windscreen and covered our faces with a mushy, semi-frozen mask.

Advance was impossible, and so we turned the machine about and came out into the bright sunshine again.

We were then flying at 4,000 feet, and the clouds were so densely compacted as to appear like mighty snow cliffs, towering miles into the air.

There was no gap or pass anywhere, so I shut off the engines and glided down, hoping to fly under them. Below the clouds snow was falling heavily, blotting out all observation beyond a few yards.

Once more we became frozen up, and, as our low elevation made flying extremely hazardous and availed us nothing, I determined to climb above the cloud-mass and, once above it, set a compass course for Lyons.

Aerial navigation is similar to navigation at sea, excepting that the indispensable sextant is more difficult to use in the air, owing to the high speed of travel and the consequent rapid change from place to place and for other technical reasons. Allowances have also to be made for the drift of the machine when side winds are blowing—an extremely difficult factor to determine accurately.

As the medium on which the machine travels is air, any active motion of that medium must necessarily have a direct influence on the machine. If, for instance, the medium on which we are travelling is a wind of 40 miles per hour, blowing directly toward our destination, and the velocity of the machine is 80 miles per hour, then the speed which the machine will travel in relation to the ground would be 120 miles per hour. If we had to forge directly ahead into the same wind, then our speed would obviously be only 40 miles per hour.

To determine the speed of a machine in relation to the ground, an instrument is fitted, called a ground-speed indicator. In side winds the machine makes leeway in addition to its forward movement, and it is the ratio of the one to the other that provides the greatest problem of aerial navigation, especially when flying above clouds or when land features are obscured.

On this particular occasion the Air Ministry had furnished us with charts indicating the trend of the winds and their approximate force at various altitudes, and so we knew, roughly, what allowances to make in our dead reckoning if we lost sight of the ground.

So we climbed steadily in a wide, ascending spiral, until we reached an altitude of 9,000 feet, and were then just above the clouds. Below us the snowstorm raged, but we had entered another world—a strange world, all our own, with bright, dazzling sunshine.

It might have been a vision of the polar regions; it undoubtedly felt like it. The mighty cloud ocean over which we were scudding resembled a polar landscape covered with snow. The rounded cloud contours might have been the domes of snow-merged summits. It was hard to conceive that that amorphous expanse was not actual, solid. Here and there flocculent towers and ramps heaved up, piled like mighty snow dumps, toppling and crushing into one another. Everything was so tremendous, so vast, that one's sense of proportion swayed uncontrolled.

Then there were tiny wisps, more delicate and frail than feathers. Chasms thousands of feet deep, sheer columns, and banks extended almost beyond eye-reach. Between us and the sun stretched isolated towers of cumulus, thrown up as if erupted from the chaos below. The sunlight, filtering through their shapeless bulk, was scattered into every conceivable gradation and shade in monotone. Round the margins the sun's rays played, outlining all with edgings of silver.

The scene was one of utter bewilderment and extravagance.

Below, the shadow of our machine pursued us, skipping from crest to crest, jumping gulfs and ridges like a bewitched phantom. Around the shadow circled a gorgeous halo, a complete flat rainbow. I have never seen anything in all my life so unreal as the solitudes of this upper world through which my companions and I were now fleeting.

My brother worked out our course, and I headed the machine on to the compass bearing for Lyons; and so away we went, riding the silver-edged sea and chased by our dancing shadow. For three hours we had no glimpse of the earth, so we navigated solely by our compass, hoping eventually to run into clear weather, or at least a break in the cloud, so that we might check our position from the world below. My brother marked our assumed position off on the chart, by dead reckoning, every fifteen minutes.

The cold grew more intense. Our hands and feet lost all feeling and our bodies became well-nigh frozen. The icy wind penetrated our thick clothing and it was with greatest difficulty that I could work the machine. Our breaths condensed on our faces and face-masks and iced up our goggles and our helmets.

Occasionally immense cloud barriers rose high above the lower cloud strata, and there was no circumventing them; these barriers were invariably charged with snow, and as I plunged the machine into them, the wings and fuselage were quickly armoured with ice. Our air-speed indicator became choked, and we ourselves were soon covered white by an accumulating layer of driving snow.

Goggles were useless, owing to the ice, and we suffered much agony through being compelled to keep a lookout with unprotected eyes—straining into the 90-miles-an-hour snow-blast.

About 1 pm. I suggested to my brother that we should have some sandwiches for lunch. On taking them from the cupboard we discovered they were frozen hard. Fortunately, we carried a thermos flask of hot coffee and the *pièce de résistance* was a few sticks of chocolate, which was part of our emergency rations. I have never felt so cold or miserable in my life as I did during those few hours. My diary is terse, if not explicit:

'This sort of flying is a rotten game. The cold is hell, and I am a silly ass for having ever embarked on the flight.'

To add to our discomfort and anxiety, we were quite uncertain as to our location, and I had visions of what would happen if we encountered a heavy side wind and got blown into the wild Atlantic.

The only really cheerful objects of the whole outfit were our two engines. They roared away and sang a deep-throated song, filled with contentment and gladness; it did not worry them that their radiator blinds, which we kept shut, were thickly coated with frozen snow.

I regarded those engines with envy. They had nice hot water circulating around them, and well, indeed, they might be happy. It seemed anomalous, too, that those engines needed water flowing around their cylinders to keep them cool, while we were sitting just a few feet away semi-frozen. I was envious! I have often thought of that day since and smiled about it—at that diary entry, and at my allusion to the two engines and my envy of their warmth.

The situation was becoming desperate. My limbs were so dead with cold that the machine was almost getting beyond my control. We must check our position and find out where we were at any cost.

Ahead loomed up a beautiful dome-shaped cloud, lined with silver edges. It was symbolical; and when all seemed dark, this rekindled in me the spark of hope. By the side of the 'cloud with the silver lining' there extended a gulf about two miles across. As we burst out over it I looked down into its abysmal depths.

At the bottom lay the world. As far as the eye could reach, in every direction stretched the illimitable cloud sea, and the only break now lay beneath us. It resembled a tremendous crater, with sides clean-cut as a shaft. Down this wonderful cloud avenue I headed the Vimy, slowly descending in a wide spiral. The escape through this marvellous gateway, seven thousand feet deep, that seemed to link the realms of the infinite with the lower world of mortals, was the most soul-stirring episode of the whole voyage.

Snow was falling heavily from the clouds that encircled us, yet down, down we went in an almost snow-free atmosphere. The omen was good; fair Fortune rode with us. The landscape was covered deep in snow, but we picked out a fairly large town, which my brother at once said was Roanne. This indicated that we were directly on our route; but it seemed too good to be true, for we had been flying at over 80 miles per hour for three hours by 'blind navigation', and had been unable to check our course.

At 1,000 feet I circled above the town. Our maps informed us that it was Roanne! Lyons, our destination, was only 40 miles away. Exquisitely indeed is the human mind constituted; for, now that we knew where we were, we all experienced that strange mental stimulus—the reaction, after mental anxiety and physical tribulation. We forgot the cold, the snow, the gloom; everything grew bright and warm with the flame of hope and success. And so eventually we reached Lyons and landed.

CHAPTER III

Lyons to Rome

I have always regarded the journey from Hounslow to Lyons as the worst stage of the flight, on account of the winter weather conditions. We had flown 510 miles on a day officially reported 'unfit for all flying'. Furthermore, we had convinced ourselves that, by careful navigation, we could fly anywhere in any sort of weather, and, what was still more, we had gained absolute confidence in our machine and engines.

We were so stiff with cold when we climbed out of the machine that we could hardly walk. But what did it matter? Our spirits ran high; we had covered the worst stage; the past would soon be forgotten, and new adventures lay awaiting us in the near, the rosy, future.

The French flying officers were very surprised when they learned we had come from London. They looked up at the weather, at the machine, then at us, and slowly shook their heads. It was an eloquent, silent expression. They were still more surprised when they learned that we intended leaving for Rome the next morning.

Not one of us could speak French very well, and we had considerable difficulty in arranging for petrol supplies to be delivered to the machine by next morning. Sergeants Bennett and Shiers just had time to look over the engines before the winter darkness settled down. We all turned into bed very early, very tired, but very happy.

On opening my personal kit that night I found it, too, had suffered the rigours of the sky journey. It was still frozen stiff—my solitary toothbrush!

Next morning was November 13th. I always hold that such a date should be banned from the months of the calendar. Daylight 6.30, cold and frosty. The petrol had not arrived at the machine, so I sent my brother Keith in search of it; his French was even less eloquent than mine. A couple of hours later he returned looking very grim, followed by 300 gallons of very servile spirit.

I explained in execrable French to a mechanic that I required 24 gallons of hot water for our radiators. It had been necessary to drain the water from the radiators the night before, owing to the low temperature; otherwise the circulating water would have been frozen into a solid block and burst the radiators. Ten minutes later the mechanic returned bearing a small jug of hot water. Our faces had been too sore to shave that morning, so I suppose he gathered from our appearance that we wanted the hot water for that purpose.

My brother Keith then had a try in that Australian tongue, famed alike for its potency and rhetoric, and universally understood throughout the breadth of the battlefields. That mechanic bowed most politely and profusely and returned in great haste, bearing triumphantly a second jug of hot water. My brother's growth, like his temper, is much more bristly than mine. While we both were literally 'losing our hair', my indispensable Bennett and Shiers had filled several petrol tins with water and had borrowed a large blow-lamp. Thus was the water heated and our tempers cooled.

We had planned overnight to leave Lyons immediately after an early breakfast, and we hoped to land at Rome well before the day closed. The delay in securing warm water for our radiators, however, meant that we were not in the air till 10 o'clock.

It was a frosty daybreak, and for a short time we encountered some clouds; but as we progressed these drifted away, clearing the atmosphere and unfolding a scene of bewildering beauty. Eastward the Alps reared up, serrating the horizon with a maze of glistening snow-peaks. Seas of cloud filled the valleys, with innumerable dark, rocky pinnacles piercing through and giving the whole scene the appearance of a rock-torn surf. Charming villas, set amidst lawns and gardens, lay tucked away over the hillsides. White roadways streaked the landscape, and close by the coast ran the thin lines of steel along which a toy-like train was passing with its burden of sight-seers to Monte Carlo and the playground of Europe.

Flying over snow-capped mountains in the Southern Alps.
[Ross and Keith Smith Collection, SLSA PRG 18/9/1/12B]

The air was keen-edged and the cold was still severe, but after the icy blasts and the spear-pointed showers of the previous day, the going was excellent. We were freed, too, from the anxiety of shaping our course by sheer navigation. Nature's great map was no longer obscured. It lay unrolled below, an enlarged edition of our own tiny charts, on which we checked its features. Picking up the River Durance quite easily, we crossed it and passed above the city of Aix; then swung east, heading for the coast and Cannes—across the famous Riviera.

Soon we caught sight of the sea. Five thousand feet below us the Mediterranean was laving the cliffs of innumerable little bays and inlets, embroidering a thin white edging of surf round their rugged bases—a narrow, white boundary-line separating green-topped cliffs from deep-blue waters.

Nice soon lay below us. The city, with its fine buildings and avenues of palms, encircled by high hills, rests on the shores of a sea of wondrous blue. It is a place of ineffable charm and peace.

A large crowd had collected on the Promenade des Anglais to witness our flight and cheer us up. We flew low enough to distinguish the doll-like figures, and though we could not return their greetings we appreciated them none the less. Then onward again with a following breeze, white-cresting the blue sea that stretched away from beneath us to the southern horizon. We circled above Monte Carlo and the famous Casino, admiring the wonderful terraces and gardens, which looked like a skilfully carved and coloured model rather than a real palace and its gardens.

We swept round, looking for a landing place, for I was inclined to test Dame Fortune and see if she would be as kind to us at the tables as she had been to us in the air. There seemed to be no suitable spot on which to land, however, so we headed on to our course again, and soon our regrets faded in admiration of the glorious coast-line over which we were speeding. Suddenly I remembered it was the 13th; Fortune had been kind to us after all.

My brother and Bennett and Shiers spent most of their time while flying along this picturesque coast in taking photographs. Kodak, Ltd, had offered a prize of £800 for the crew of the machine who produced the best 50 negatives taken during the Australian flight. We entered for this prize and eventually won it and Kodak's had supplied us with their cameras and dozens of films.

Mentone, nestling in its bay, was the last glimpse we had of France; then, still following the railway line that runs along the coast, we crossed the border into Italy without trouble from the customs officials. Less than half an hour later we passed San Remo and, instead of following the coast-line north, I kept the Vimy headed almost due east, and, crossing the Gulf of Genoa, picked up the coast again at Spezia and turned south once more. Here we met a strong head wind, and this, added to the handicap of our delayed start, made it evident that we could not reach Rome before dark.

I knew that there was an aerodrome at Pisa, since it was one of the stations on the air route to Egypt, so decided to spend the night there and go on to Rome early next day. It was well down the afternoon when we picked out the aerodrome, and the ground looked very wet and desolate as we circled above it. But we landed successfully through a whirl of mud and water, whisked up by the propellers.

As we taxied across the slippery 'drome toward the hangars, several Italian flying officers came out to greet us. They were profusely polite, and while our scholarship boasted 'little French and less Italian', there was no doubt about their cordial welcome and their curiosity. By means of that universal language of gesture, in which these Latins are so accomplished, they made us at home and indicated that an English officer was stationed in Pisa and that we might reach him by telephone.

After considerable trouble I managed to have him called up and asked him to come down to the aerodrome. I was delighted to find that the officer was Captain Horne, of the Royal Air Force, who had been appointed to the air-route station. Accommodation for our party was promptly arranged, and after attending to the machine we motored into Pisa and stayed the night at an hotel.

Heavy rain set in, and when we were awakened in the morning it was still pouring, with a strong slant from the south. In spite of the unsuitable condition, we decided to go down to the aerodrome and, if possible, get up and go on to Rome that day.

On our arrival at the hangars we found, to our dismay, that the aerodrome looked more like a lake than a landing ground. However, I started up the engines and endeavoured to taxi into the wind, but the machine became badly bogged, the wheels refusing to budge an inch.

A force of thirty Italian mechanics came to help us, but it took us an hour and a half to extricate the machine. Our difficulties in getting anything like 'teamwork' were increased by our lack of knowledge of Italian, and Sergeant Bennett amused us greatly by breaking into Arabic, with all the French he knew sifted in. A second attempt also resulted in failure, and by the time the machine had been dug out I came to the conclusion that it was hopeless to try to leave that day. It was still raining, so we covered up the engines and reluctantly returned to the town, soaking wet and grimed with mud.

Late in the afternoon the rain ceased, so my brother and I went sight-seeing. We visited the usual hackneyed tourist sites, including the famous Leaning Tower. Sergeant Shiers had never seen this Tower before and his first remark was: 'Well, I reckon the architect who designed the damned thing must have had a bit too much Johnny Walker'.

Elections were in progress and the whole town swayed with excitement. We attracted much attention walking about in uniform; for, besides Captain Horne, we were the only British officers in Pisa.

We were cheerful, for we had hopes that the water would drain off the aerodrome by the following morning, but once more we awoke to disappointment. Drizzling rain and a cold south wind ushered in the new day. However, we went down to the aerodrome, determined to get the machine into the air somehow.

My brother and I walked over the aerodrome, stamping in the mud to try to find a hard track for the machine. We got very wet, but managed to find a pathway with a fairly hard surface.

All went well until I swung the machine round, just preparatory to opening the engines full out for getting off. In doing this sharp turn, one wheel became a pivot in the mud and stuck fast; so once more we were badly bogged. Our Italian friends came to the rescue again, and by digging and pulling got the machine out of the hole which it had made for itself. The ground was so soft that the wheels began to sink in slowly, and I realised that if we were to get off at all it must be at once.

I opened out the engines, but the machine would not move forward, as the wheels had become embedded in the mud; on the other hand, the tail lifted off the ground and there was the danger of the machine standing up on its nose. To overcome this difficulty

Sergeant Bennett applied the whole of his weight on to the tail-plane, and I once more opened the engines full out. Some of the Italian mechanics pulled forward on the wing-tips, and this time the machine started to move forward slowly. I suddenly realised that Bennett was not on board, but as I had got the machine moving at last, I was afraid to stop her again.

I felt sure that he would clamber on board somehow, as I had previously told him that as soon as the machine started to move he would have to make a flying jump for it or else take the next train to Rome.

We gathered very rapidly, and, after leaving the ground, I was delighted to see Sergeant Bennett on board when I looked round. The take-off was very exciting and hazardous, as the Vimy had to plough her way through soft mud and water. The water was sucked up and whirled around by the propellers, so that we became soaked through and plastered with liquid mud. I am sure that in a cinema picture our performance would resemble the take-off of a seaplane more than that of a land machine rising from an aerodrome. We were tremendously relieved to find the freedom of our wings again, and though we laughed at our discomfiture, it was certainly a providential take-off and one that I should not care to repeat. We afterward learned that we had been doubly lucky, for the rain continued to fall in torrents for the next week and the aerodrome was temporarily impossible.

Our flight toward Rome was one long battle against heavy head winds and through dense clouds. We had been in the air barely an hour when the oil gauge on one of the engines dropped to zero.

Thinking that something had gone wrong with the lubricating system I switched off this engine and flew along close to the ground on the other engine, looking closely for a place to land. Fortunately we were not far from the Italian aerodrome at Venturina, and there I landed.

Sergeant Shiers quickly discovered that the fault was in the gauge itself, and not in the lubricating system, and it was only a matter of minutes before we were in the air again. The wind had increased, and the rest of the voyage to Rome was boisterous and unpleasant. Our average ground speed was a bare fifty miles an hour, so that it was not till late in the afternoon that we were above the city of the Caesars.

In spite of the fatigue induced by our strenuous experiences of the day and our eagerness to get down to earth, I could not help being stirred by the beauty of the historic city. The sun was peering through the space between the clouds and the distant mountain tops and, slanting across the city, gave it an appearance of majestic splendour. In this soft evening light, Rome reflected something of its old glory. Details were subdued, so that much of the ugliness of its modern constructions was softened. Below, 'the Yellow Tiber', spanned by numerous bridges, curved its muddy course out into the twilight and to the sea.

In the brief space of a few minutes we had circled the city within the walls, and it was with feelings of relief that we landed at the Centocelle aerodrome. A hospitable welcome was accorded us by the commandant of the Italian Flying Corps and by the British air attaché. The latter kindly attended to our wants, had a military guard placed over the machine and acted as interpreter.

CHAPTER IV

Rome to Cairo

My original plan was to make the next stage a non-stop flight from Rome to Athens, thence to Cairo in another flight. This decision was the result of a report received in England that the aerodrome at Suda Bay, on the northern side of Crete, was flooded and would be unfit for landing till after winter. The air attaché at Rome, however, told me that the Suda Bay aerodrome was still in good condition, but that I could make sure by dropping down at Taranto and inquiring at the British aerodrome there.

A glance at the map will show that the Cretan route saves a considerable distance, Suda Bay providing a half-way house. I therefore decided at once to take the Taranto course and try to save the long stretch of Mediterranean from Athens to Cairo.

After daylight, we left Rome in very bad weather. Our route for the first few miles followed the Appian Way, and as we were flying low we had a fine view of this ancient highway. The landscape for the most part was obscured by broken clouds, but through the rifts we had fleeting glimpses of the wild and spectacular nature below us.

Naples was not directly on our course to Taranto, but having visited it previously as a tourist, I made a detour in order to photograph and gaze down upon its wondrous bay from the sky. To my intense disappointment, clouds and mist robbed us of my desire, and even the mighty Vesuvius was buried somewhere beneath the sea of clouds;

so, reluctantly, I turned away and resumed our course to Taranto.

Our course now lay almost due east across the Apennines; but here again the clouds had banked against the mountains, and only an occasional peak peered through them. Owing to the clouds and my scant knowledge of the country, I determined to fly low, following, more or less, the course of the valleys, which were nearly cloud-free.

From breaks in the clouds, the sun beamed down on to vales of great loveliness. Numerous small waterfalls dashed down the mountain sides, and streams like silver threads rippled away through the valleys. The lower steps of the mountains were terraced, and wherever a flat stretch of soil presented itself, small homesteads nestled, surrounded by cultivation. Sometimes we would be only a few hundred feet above the ground when crossing the crest of a ridge; then we would burst out over a valley several thousand feet deep.

Flying became extremely difficult at this stage, owing to the bumpy nature of the atmosphere. At times the machine was literally tossed about like a leaf, and for three-quarters of an hour we experienced some of the roughest flying conditions of the whole journey. On one occasion our altimeter did a drop of 1,000 feet, and bumps of 400 and 500 feet, both upward and downward, were frequent. I can only attribute this aerial disturbance to the rough nature of the country and the proximity of clouds to the mountain tops.

A strong following wind was blowing, and I was very much relieved when we got clear of the mountains and were following the coast down to Taranto. The town of Taranto presents a busy scene from the air. A great number of ships and transports were anchored off shore, and as the air had now cleared somewhat, we had a glorious view of this great Mediterranean seaport, which played such an important part in the Eastern campaign. We could still discern long lines of tents in the British camp, and everywhere there was the great activity which characterises a military centre.

The town is small and picturesquely situated at the head of a little inland bay, which forms a magnificent natural harbour. Below us the boom protecting the entrance from submarines was clearly discernible.

When we landed we were greeted by a number of officers of the Royal Air Force who were stationed there, as Taranto at that time was one of the main aerodromes on the route from London to Cairo.

The machine was pegged down and lashed, and after an excellent lunch at the officers' mess we spent the afternoon working on the engines and preparing for the flight across the sea to Crete the following day. The British camp was particularly well kept, and in front of headquarters there was a fine garden with chrysanthemums in full bloom.

Here I met many comrades with whom I had been associated during the war. This meeting was a pleasant relaxation from the mental strain of the past few days, and I gleaned much valuable information about the aerodrome at Suda Bay. I was delighted to learn that it was still in good condition and was in charge of Royal Air Force personnel. This information finally decided me to cancel the idea of flying on to Athens. I now determined to fly to Suda Bay, thus cutting the long sea flight of the Mediterranean into two shorter sections and saving upwards of 200 miles.

After a good night's rest in comfortable beds, we were up at our usual hour and made an early start for Suda Bay.

Once again the weather was cruel to us. First, we flew east to the heel of Italy, and then headed across the open sea to the island of Corfu. Low clouds and rain forced us down to 800 feet above the sea. The flight was miserable. The driving rain cut our faces and obscured all distant vision. Almost before we realised it, Corfu loomed up in the mist, and so I altered the course to southeast and flew down the coast of Greece.

The bad weather made our voyage down this rugged coast very hazardous, and on one occasion, after passing through a particularly low bank of cloud, I was terrified to observe a rocky island loom up in the mist directly ahead. It was only by turning sharply at right angles that I avoided crashing the machine against its precipitous sides.

All this time we were flying at a height of no more than 800 feet, and so it was with intense relief that we reached Cape Matea, the most southern point of Greece, and headed across the sea to Crete.

The clouds now lifted, and the mists dissipated, unfolding a scene of rare enchantment. The high ranges of Crete soon loomed up before us. A layer of cloud encircled the island like a great wreath. The mountains rose nobly above it, and the coast, rocky and surf-beaten, could be seen below. All this, set in a sea of wondrous blue, bathed in bright sunshine, lay before us. It was a gladsome and welcome sight.

Wheeling above the town of Canea, which is on the opposite side of a narrow neck to Suda Bay, we soon located the aerodrome and circled above it preparatory to landing.

The aerodrome is not of the best and is rather a tricky place for negotiating a landing, being surrounded on three sides by high, rocky hills; but we succeeded in making a good landing. Here, too, we were welcomed by an officer of the Royal Air Force and a small crowd of inhabitants, who gathered round the machine, examining it—and us with curious interest.

With the knowledge that on the morrow our longest oversea flight, in this half of the voyage, awaited us, we spent most of the afternoon in a particularly thorough overhaul of the machine, and then accepted our RAF friend's invitation to look over the town and take tea at his house. We found Canea to be an extremely picturesque and interesting old place. Its massive castle walls, its narrow cobbled streets, and its quaint, old-fashioned, but substantial buildings, reminiscent of a bygone age, are all in keeping with its history, which runs back to the Christian era, and its legends, which run back a league or two further.

Our pilot excited our admiration by the expert way in which he steered us through a maze of rough-surfaced alleyways, our Ford causing a great scattering of children and dogs—both of which appear to thrive here in large numbers.

Eventually he conducted us to a quaint little cafe—a sort of tavern, at which the people seem by custom to foregather for a cup of coffee before dinner. The café-au-lait was excellent, and, as our host racily recounted his experiences, I came to the conclusion that life in Canea, small and isolated as it is, holds compensations, and is not nearly as dull as it appears at first glance.

The short run home to our RAF friend's house was certainly not monotonous, but we arrived undamaged and undamaging. Since the house was rather small to accommodate unexpected guests, we cheerfully agreed to sleep in the small British hospital close by. We turned in early, planning to take a good night's rest and get away betimes in the morning.

A few minutes after putting out the lights, I heard my brother tossing about in bed, and called out to know if anything ailed him. 'Yes,' he said, 'I fancy I'm getting prickly heat.'[1] A few minutes later

---

1   Also known as heat rash, and caused by high heat and humidity.

I got a touch of it myself, and, bounding out of bed, reached for the candle. The beds were full of prickly heat! 'Prickly heat' held the fort in large and hungry battalions.

We retreated and spent the night curled up on the floor of an adjoining room. When we turned out we found that it had been raining heavily and the air was still thick with drizzle. The prospect was not good for crossing the island, which, though only a few miles wide, is intersected by an irregular range of mountains, of which the famous Mount Ida is one of the several peaks. But, with our experience of the muddy aerodrome at Pisa fresh in our minds, we decided to get aloft as soon as possible rather than risk the ground, which was already becoming soft and degenerating into a bog.

We took off quite easily, and soon after leaving the ground encountered a layer of cloud, but pushed through and out—only to find ourselves beneath another stratum. Our charted route lay southeast, then south, with the southernmost point of the island as the objective, and I had been told that it was easy to follow a rough track leading from Canea through a pass in the mountains; but, with clouds above and below, it was not so easy.

I decided to try to locate the pass in the hope of getting through without the necessity of climbing above the mountains, and so wasting valuable time. Fortune favoured us. I found the pass and to my joy discovered that there was just sufficient room for us to scrape over the top without entering the cloud. We appeared to be only a few feet above the rocks when we cleared the crest, but it was preferable to having to barge blindly through the clouds, running the consequent risk of hitting a mountain crag.

On the southern side of the ranges the air was much clearer, and we were soon flying over the coast-line. We took observations and set a compass course for Sollum, on the African coast. Two hundred and fifty miles of open sea had to be crossed. Before we started Bennett and Shiers had given a final look over the engines, which had been running perfectly, and almost the last thing they did before climbing aboard was to inflate the four spare inner tubes of our landing wheels; they would make first-class life-buoys if we had to come down between Crete and Africa.

I would have preferred flying at about 5,000 feet, but our enemies, the clouds, which ever harassed us, forced us to fly at an altitude of from 1,500 to 2,000 feet above the face of the sea. There was a light, favouring wind, and the going was smooth and even; but as the land dropped behind, and mile after mile was flown, one began to realise the meaning of the term, 'a waste of waters'.

On and on we flew, yet, save for the wind of our own passage through the air, could scarcely tell that we were moving; for, unlike the flight across the land and down the seacoast, there was nothing by which to gauge our movement. The cloud roof was dull and uninteresting; the sea-floor grey, desolate, and empty as far as the eye could reach.

My brother took out his case and began writing letters. I studied the charts and the compass and kept the machine on the course. Then suddenly, a little to the right of the course, appeared a minute object that separated into two as we drew nearer, and finally resolved itself into a pair of vessels linked together with a tow-line. Very tiny they looked down there and very lonely.

We were heading for Sollum, on the African coast, 250 miles from Crete, as the 'plane flies. I wondered if these ships were making the same port, and how long it would take them to do the journey that we were counting on accomplishing in about four hours. I felt quite sorry for the poor midgets toiling along with their tow-rope, and speculated on what would happen if a big sea got up. Doubtless they looked up at us—they must have heard our engines booming—and wondered, too. Perhaps they envied us our wings; perhaps they pitied us and congratulated themselves on the sound decks beneath their feet.

Ten minutes and they were far behind us; another ten and they were out of sight; but they had, without knowing it, cheered us immensely. They proved the only speck of life we saw on all that area of waters. Once more we entered the loneliness of sea and sky, but we had the sense of having passed a definite point, and now we kept a keen lookout for land.

Our first glimpse of Africa was of a barren, desert coast-line, but it was a welcome sight none the less. On reaching Sollum we turned and flew along the coast as far as Mersa Matruh. The land below was flat and uninteresting desert, with nothing to relieve the monotony. Without landing at Mersa Matruh, we headed direct for Cairo, across the grey-brown sea of sand, passing over Wadi Natrum, which is merely a cluster of straggling palms beside a salt-pan.

We were not sorry to descry those landmarks of the ages, the Pyramids, and soon we could pick out the minarets and mosques of the Egyptian capital itself. Now we were winging our way over Old Father Nile and across landmarks that were as familiar to me as the Heliopolis aerodrome itself, to which destination I was guiding the Vimy.

No wonder I glanced affectionately over the silent engines as we came to rest. I felt extremely happy as we sat there a moment or two, waiting for the fellows to come up and welcome us. We had come through from Suda Bay, a distance of 650 miles, in a non-stop flight of seven and a half hours, thus completing the first and worst of the four stages into which I had divided the total journey. That bit of route from London to Cairo—pioneered in 1917 by my old commanding officer, General Borton—had taken its toll, and I had been more than a little afraid of it on account of the possibility of bad weather and my ignorance of the country and the aerodromes. And here we were, safe, with our machine as sound as when she started.

A familiar stage, with all the prospects of fine weather, lay before us. There was some excuse for a flash of thankfulness and exultation. Then the boys were greeting us, and a rousing welcome it was from men with whom I had served during the war. Our mechanics, too, found old comrades who hauled them off to celebrate the occasion before attending to the engines.

It was quite like old times to climb into a car, to spin through well-known thoroughfares to Shepheard's, to sink luxuriantly into the arms of a great and familiar lounge chair, and to yarn over the events that had happened since last I occupied it.

Aerial view of the pyramids at Giza, near Cairo, Egypt, the location of the finish for the 6th leg of the England–Australia air race. [Ross and Keith Smith Collection, SLSA PRG 18/9/1/13A]

My friends tried to persuade me to attend a dance that was being held there that night, but I needed all the sleep I could get, and so declined reluctantly. But for an hour or more I sat in an easy chair on the well-known verandah, and listened to the sweet strains of the music inside, and that other strange blend of street cries—veritable kaleidoscope of sound—that may be heard nowhere save in Cairo. I noted, too, the beauty and chivalry coming in, and watched the curious procession of all sorts passing by.

I had to shake myself to be assured that it was not a splendid and fantastic dream. As we lounged there a messenger boy brought a cable for me—we had sent our own messages off long before. It was from General Borton, congratulating us on our safe arrival in Egypt and wishing us good luck for the next stage.

While I was reading this kind remembrance from my old CO, an Arab paper boy came crying his wares, and I bought a news-sheet and read with amused interest the story of our doings during the last few days. I also read, with a shock of keen regret, of the accident that had befallen our gallant competitors, Lieutenants Douglas and Ross, who had both been killed practically at the starting-post, just a few days after we left, through the crashing of their machine.[2] Then we turned to the column that recorded the progress of Monsieur Poulet, who had left Paris thirty days before and who, we saw by the cables, was now in India.

We had certainly gained a good deal on the Frenchman, but he still held a big lead, and we were keen to get on with the next stage. We turned in that night feeling happier and more rested than at any moment since we left England, and we slept like proverbial tops.

---

2 Roger Douglas and Leslie Ross had taken off in their single-engined Alliance aircraft named *Endeavour* on the day after the Vimy left Hounslow, crashing within minutes of departure and killing both men.

CHAPTER V

Cairo to Bagdad

We had intended staying a day in Cairo to rest, but, owing to the day we lost at Pisa, we were now one day behind our scheduled time; so I decided that it must be made up. There had been a heavy fog over night, and on our arrival at the aerodrome the weather conditions were not at all enticing. Telegraphic reports from Palestine indicated 'Weather conditions unsuited for flying'.

My inclinations wavered. We were at a hospitable aerodrome, surrounded by old friends; rain had begun to fall and we were all very tired. The Vimy, however, had been overhauled the night before and everything stood ready. Perhaps at the end of the journey we would be more limb-weary, and a single day might discount the success of the venture; so I made up my mind to proceed.

We took off from Heliopolis aerodrome with the cheers of my old war comrades sounding above our engines. For fifty miles we followed the Ismailia Canal to Tel-el-Kebir. The banks were bordered by a patchwork of densely cultivated and irrigated lands; beyond, arid barrenness, sand, and nothing.

On the canal the great white lateen sails of dhows and feluccas in large number resembled a model yacht regatta. It was all very beautiful and wonderful. Northward the waterways, canals, and lakes of the Nile delta stood out like silver threads woven around the margins of patches in a patch-quilt, for the sun had now burst through the clouds, and all the world sprang into life and light. From aloft, without the sun, the world is a gloomy looking place, doleful and dead.

Over the famous old battlefield of 1882—Tel-el Kebir—where Arabi Pasha suffered ignominiously by the valour of British arms, even now there was a camp of British and Indian cavalry.[1]

And soon to the canal that links north with south—a straight cut of deep-blue water, running to the horizon transversely to our course—and ahead the grey desert sands, only limited by the blue sky.

Below, a P. and O. steamer, heading south, passes down the Suez Canal. Perhaps she is bound for Australia; she will call in at Adelaide, my home and destination! With a smile, I contrasted the old and the new methods of transportation, and a throb of exultation thrilled us all. Still, we wondered—unspoken the thoughts—who would reach Australia first.

Kantara[2] now lay below us, that vast series of store-dumps—a mushroom city beneath canvas which had sprung into being since the British occupation of Palestine, and from which practically all commissariat and munition supplies were drawn. As we passed over Kantara, feelings of confidence, mingled with no small satisfaction, filled me. We were now entering upon country I knew as well as my own homeland, for I had spent six months traversing it with the Australian Light Horse before I started flying; furthermore, I had been over the entire air route which now lay before us, as far as Java.

---

1 Arabi or Urābi Pasha—in full Ahmad ʾUrābi Pasha al-Misri—was an Egyptian nationalist whose army was defeated at Tel-el Kebir in September 1882 by British troops under the command of Sir Garnet Wolseley.

2 El Qantara

Aerial view of the Suez Canal at Kantara (El Qantara), Egypt,
18 November 1919, the location of the finish for the 6th leg of the England–
Australia air race. [Ross and Keith Smith Collection, SLSA PRG 18/9/1/11H]

The section from Hounslow to Cairo I had always regarded with some trepidation, on account of the winter storms and bad weather. Now we could look forward to improving atmospheric conditions and good aerodromes as far as Calcutta at least. This enabled us to view more rosily the ultimate issue.

Kantara soon lay beyond the rolling eternity of sand which all who served through the rigours and privations of the desert campaign call 'Hell'. It was somewhere in these regions that the Children of Israel wandered for forty years. Forty minutes in the Vimy was quite sufficient for us. We looked down upon that golden sea of desolation, with only here and there a solitary clump of date palms that boasts the name oasis, and we felt very sympathetic toward the Children of Israel. Two things alone stood out clearly in the wilderness—the iron way, which had been thrust forward to carry supplies from Kantara to the fighting front, and the line of water-main beside it.

We were flying at an altitude of 1,500 feet, so that it was possible to pick out all details readily. As we passed over the old battlefield of Romani, I picked out my old camping site and machine-gun nests.

El-Arish,[3] Rafa, Gaza—all came into being; then out over the brim of the world of sand. Gaza from the air is as pitiful a sight as it is from the ground. In its loneliness and ruin, an atmosphere of great sadness has descended upon it. On the site of a once prosperous town stands war's memorial—a necropolis of shattered buildings. The trenches before Gaza and on the hill Ali Muntar looked as though they had been but recently vacated.

---

3   Arish or el Arīsh, the largest town on the Sinai Peninsula.

Next we passed over the Medjdel aerodrome,[4] and as I gazed down at the marks where the hangars had stood, many memories of bygone days came pleasantly back to me. Soon after leaving Medjdel we ran into dense clouds, and on reaching Ramleh[5] heavy rain began to fall. There was an RAF squadron station on the old aerodrome, and I was sorely tempted to land and renew old friendships, for I had been stationed at this aerodrome for five months at the latter end of the war. However, this was no joy-ride; so I reluctantly passed over this haven of refuge, and then once more out into the bleak world of storm and rain; but I was much cheered by the whole squadron turning out on to their aerodrome and waving up to us.

My past experiences in Palestine rainstorms steeled me for what was to follow, and from Ramleh to the Sea of Galilee the weather was despicable and smote us relentlessly. The torrential rain cut our faces and well-nigh blinded us. We were soaked through and miserably cold. One thing only comforted me, and that was the merry song of the engines. Whether 'in breeze or gale or storm', they heeded not. On through the rain and wrack they bore us, as in the times of warmth and sunshine, singing their deep-throated song—'All goes well!'

Fortunately I knew the country very well, for after passing Nazareth I had to follow the winding course of the valleys, owing to low clouds, until the Jordan was reached.

The River Jordan presented an extraordinary sight. The main stream has eroded a narrow channel between wide banks, down which its waters meander in an aimless way, zig-zagging a serpentine course across a forbidding plain of great barrenness and desolation. A narrow green belt, sombre in colour and age, pursues the river

---

4   Medjdel or Magdala, an ancient city on the shore of the Sea of Galilee.
5   Also Ramla or Rama.

through the Jordan Valley, which for the greater part is an arid waste, speckled with sparse and stunted shrubs. The river enters the Dead Sea at nearly 1,300 feet below the level of the Mediterranean.

The Sea of Galilee is, roughly, 700 feet above Dead Sea level, and, as we were flying 500 feet above the river, most of our journey through the Jordan Valley was done at an elevation several hundred feet below the level of the ocean.

On reaching the Sea of Galilee the weather improved. As we passed over the great lake, where deep-green waters rest in a bowl encompassed by abrupt hills, strange emotions passed over me, for below us lay a hallowed place—a scene of ineffable charm, peace, and sanctity.

I now headed the Vimy northeast for Damascus and climbed up to 5,000 feet. Occasional cloud patches passed below us, but the landscape for the most part was drear and featureless, save for a line of snow-clad summits that lay away to the north, Mount Hermon and the Anti-Lebanon Mountains. The flight through Palestine had been an ordeal; extreme weariness gripped us all, for we were still soaking wet and very cold.

Then once more joy filled our thankful hearts when our straining eyes picked up Damascus, a miraged streak on the horizon of a desert wilderness. The streak became irregular. It grew into a band assuming height and breadth, minute excrescences, and well-defined contours. Colour crept in; details resolved, developed, enlarged; a city arose from out the waste of sands, an oasis, glorious, magical, enchanting—this was Damascus. A city almost ethereal in its beauty, rearing a forest of slender minarets and cupolas, surrounded by dense groves and woods, had sprung into being, as if by magic, from the Syrian desert.

Although one of the world's most ancient cities, age has dealt lightly with Damascus. From the air it appears no older than the blaze of poplars and cypresses that features the gardens and shades the sun-baked mud-houses and mosques. Beyond the city, beautiful gardens and glades extend, gradually dwindling and blending into the desert spaces. To the north and west rise the multi-coloured foothills of the Anti-Lebanon Mountains, flanked by the higher peaks with radiant snow mantlings.

Damascus invited and offered a haven of rest. Great was our joy on touching the ground; greater still to be welcomed by old comrades, and to be cared for. The Vimy, too, was looked after. Bennett and Shiers attended to their beloved engines, while I overhauled the controls, and my brother Keith filled up with 'Shell', to be ready for an early start on the morrow.

After attending to the machine, we drove in another machine—a Ford—into Damascus and took lodgings at the leading hotel, where the fare was excellent and sleep undisturbed by the parasites common to the country. Damascus is wholly Oriental, though in many ways it is adopting Western fashions and customs. Trams run in the city, and though their speed harmonizes with the indolent habits of the Orient, they seem strangely out of place, as also does the electric light that sheds its beams of searching and misplaced effulgence in the bazaars and squalid stalls, where shadow, deep shadow, is essential to effect a successful sale.

I looked out of my window before turning in. A myriad spires, misty and intangible, pointed to a heaven brilliant with stars: a faint breeze drifted in from the desert. The atmosphere was laden with mystery and enchantment. I felt contented. The skies promised sunshine, and henceforth the weather would be good!

Conceive my dismay when, on awakening with the morning, I discovered heavy rain falling: still further was I dismayed to find the aerodrome surface rapidly becoming soft, and the wheels of the Vimy sinking in. As there was no sign of the weather clearing up, we greased our tyres to assist their passage through the sticky clay, started up the engines, and, to my unspeakable relief, the Vimy moved ahead.

But the take-off was not lacking in excitement. The propellers sucked up water and mud, whirling in all directions (we happened to be included in one of them), and so we rose into the air, once more to be cut by the lash of the elements. To my intense relief, the storm did not extend more than a score of miles beyond Damascus.

We were now heading for Tadmur; again the desert extended before us—a rolling expanse of dreary grey sand over which it was some satisfaction to speed at eighty-five miles per hour. Tadmur is a miserable village of mud huts that has sprung up amidst the noble ruins of ancient Palmyra.[6] The modern bazaars are built for shelter among the ancient columns and fragmentary walls of the Temple of the Sun. These magnificent ruins are the bleached skeletons of a glorious past, austere and dignified even in the squalor and meanness that surround them. From Tadmur the route lay east to Abu Kemal,[7] on the Euphrates.

Two hours later we observed an encampment consisting of several hundred black goat-hair tents, and gathered around them were vast herds of camels. As we were flying low at the time, our sudden appearance caused a stampede, not only among the beasts, but also the occupants of the tents. They decamped, evidently terror-stricken.

6   Palmyra is in central Syria.
7   Abu Kamal or Al-Bukamal is in eastern Syria near the modern-day border with Iraq.

We subsequently learned that the camels were the spoils of a victorious raid. Perhaps the raiders thought we were the Judgment!

On reaching Abu Kemal we turned southeast, following down the course of the Euphrates. It was a pleasant change, after the interminable desert, to pursue the lazy course of the great river and to pass again over fertile tracts and numerous villages.

The most remarkable of these villages is Hit, not only on account of the ancient city which lies buried here, but because there are several bitumen springs, from which this valuable commodity oozes in vast quantities. Practically every native who owns a boat on the Euphrates has copied Noah, who was commanded to 'pitch the ark within and without with pitch'.

On leaving Abu Kemal we encountered strong head winds, which diminished our speed considerably. I was becoming anxious as to whether we could reach Bagdad before dark, as I was not keen to make a night landing there.

The sun was fast sinking in the west, and as we flew over Ramadie[8] it dipped below the horizon. I decided that there would not be time to do the forty miles to Bagdad before dark. We selected a suitable landing ground among some old trenches, close to a cavalry camp, and landed.

We had landed on the old Ramadie battlefield, which was one of the notable sites of the Mesopotamian campaign. Soon after landing the CO of the Indian cavalry regiment came out to greet us, and proffered the hospitality of his camp.

We were delighted to learn there was a small supply of aviation petrol here, and we obtained sufficient to carry us through to Basra

---

8   Ramadi is in central Iraq. During World War I two Battles of Ramadi were fought between British and Ottoman forces in July and September 1917.

Sunset behind the Vickers Vimy at Ramadi, near Baghdad, 30 November 1919. [Ross and Keith Smith Collection, SLSA PRG 18/7/6]

without having to land at Bagdad. An Indian guard was mounted over the machine, and the Vimy was securely lashed down for the night.

The CO of the 10th Indian Lancers and his staff were thoroughly pleased to see us, and over the excellent dinner that was prepared we told the latest happenings in London—their home: They were a fine, stout-hearted lot of fellows and greatly we appreciated their hospitality. We felt truly sorry for them stationed in such a remote, isolated place as Ramadie.

About 11 o'clock that night a heavy windstorm swooped down upon us, and my brother and myself rushed out to the machine. The wind had suddenly changed, and was now blowing hard on the tail of the machine. The Vimy was in imminent danger of being blown over and crashed.

We turned out fifty men from the nearest camp. They hung on to the machine until we started up the engines and swung her head round into the wind. It was a pitch-dark night, and the gale whirled the sand into blinding eddies, cutting our faces and eyes. One very severe gust caught one of the ailerons and snapped the top balance-wires. This allowed all four ailerons to flap about in a very dangerous manner, and it looked as though they would all be wrenched off before we could secure them.

By weight of arms, however, we eventually managed to secure the ailerons before serious damage was done. At last the machine was turned, facing the wind, and in that position successfully weathered the storm. Throughout the rest of the night the guard hung on to the machine and all stood by.

The storm abated by morning. We found that all the aileron control wires were strained or broken. The sand had choked up everything exposed to the weather, and by the time the damage had been repaired and our tanks filled with petrol it was noon.

For the first time since leaving London we had promise of a good flying day with a following wind. This good fortune atoned for our troubles of the night and for our lack of sleep. We were sweeping along at 100 miles an hour, and in less than thirty minutes Bagdad lay below. Glorious old Bagdad! Bagdad today, faded of all its old glory, is a place of poverty and decay, alluring only through name and association. Yet, in spite of its meanness and squalor, the magic city of Haroun-al-Raschid, the hero of the Arabian Nights, of Aladdin, and Sinbad the Sailor, shall remain immortal.

CHAPTER VI

Over Mesopot to Karachi

It is hard to believe that the land above which we were now speeding was once the garden of the world. Oh, where is thy wealth and prosperity, fair Babylonia? Despoiled by the ravages of the Ottoman Empire, misruled and wasted by the accursed methods of the Turkish Government, it seems incredible that this void of marsh and waste land was once a country of milk and honey, a land of pomp and luxury that led the civilization of the world.

From a height, the aspect of Bagdad is more inviting than from the ground. A maze of narrow streets, wandering through a tesselated plan of flat roofs, of spires and green splashes of cultivation and date palms, of a great muddy brown river, covered with innumerable little round dots, which on closer investigation resolve themselves into circular tub-like boats—all this is Bagdad, and the impression is pleasing and reminiscent of bygone glory.

There is but one thoroughfare that stands pre-eminent to-day in Bagdad—a wide road which the Turks had cut through the city to make way for the retreat of their routed army before the victorious British under General Maude; and so now may we see the dawn of a new era and fairer days ahead for this outcast land.

Every mile of land and river above which we were passing was a measure of history of valorous effort, mighty deeds, and heroism.

The map of Mesopotamia unrolled before us. Here lay the old battlefields of Ctesiphon, Laff, Tubal, the trench systems still being clearly observable.

Kut el Amara,[1] where was enacted the most dramatic and heroic episode of the Mesopotamian campaign, next came into view. For five awful months that little garrison of British men, led and cheered by their beloved general, had held out against the Turk, disease, and the pangs of starvation. The glorious story of the defence of Kut and the surrender is one of those splendid episodes that thrill the heart of every Englishman, and which shall live immortal with the memories of Lucknow, Delhi, Khartoum, Ladysmith, and Mafeking.

In describing Mesopotamia I am inclined to quote the terse, if ineloquent, account of the British Tommy who wrote of it: 'A hell of a place, with two big rivers and miles and miles of dam all between them.' Yet the possibilities of development are infinite and the potentialities golden—a land of suspended fertility, where animation and prosperity lie for the time dormant—a wondrous garden where centuries of neglect and rapine have reaped desolation and barrenness. The land is athirst, but the two great rivers, the Tigris and the Euphrates, move sullenly on, ebbing their life out to the sea. Turn back these tides into the veins of irrigation and the land will be replenished, Eden shall be again, and even the valley of the Nile shall be despised to it.

Exulting in the fair weather and following breeze, we swept over the world at 100 miles an hour. Three thousand feet below, the

---

1   Kut al Amara, or Al-Kūt, is located in eastern Iraq, about 160 kilometres south east of Baghdad. The Siege of Kut Al Amara from December 1915 to April 1916, also known as the First Battle of Kut, has been described as the worst defeat of the Allies in World War I.

two great rivers conflux and unite in the Shatt-el-Arab,[2] with the miserable village of Kurnah at the junction—a village built of mud, and its humanity of the same colour as the turbid streams that bear the soil of Asia Minor away to the Persian Gulf.

Clusters of date palms and a scant belt of vegetation fringe the bank, but beyond a half mile or so there is nothing but the dun-coloured wilderness, the miraged sky-line, and the blue canopy where the sun rules king.

All this once was the Garden of Eden. Today it is not a delectable site: but who may speak of the morrow? The waters of the Shatt-el-Arab, heavily impregnated with mud, resemble the outflow from a mud geyser, swirling and boiling; they move oozily forward as their caprice inclines, the silt is precipitated, shallows form, mud-banks come into being, grow into islets, and disappear with the next flood.

The flight from Bagdad to Basra took just under three hours. The crazy river barge, probing its way through shallows, rips, and mud, generally takes a fortnight! Basra we discovered to be a hive of activity. It was the main shipping port during the Mesopotamian campaign, and a large military base and aerodrome were still in evidence. The aerodrome stretches to the horizon, and with the British camp extends for miles along the eastern bank.

We crossed over to the town in one of the characteristic river boats called mahailas—a Viking vessel strangely and crudely carved at prow and stern, and with sails as multi-patched as the garments of the crew. The town is an unlovely place of strange and vari-odorous perfumes; so after dispatching mails we hastened back to the Vimy.

---

2   The Shatt al-Arab or Arvand Rud is a river formed by the confluence of the Euphrates and the Tigris in southern Iraq.

An armed guard around the Vickers Vimy at Basra, Iraq,
to discourage souvenir hunters, 22–23 November 1919.
[Ross and Keith Smith Collection, SLSA PRG 18/7/7]

As there was a Royal Air Force depôt here, I decided to delay a day
and allow Bennett and Shiers to overhaul and adjust the engines.

There was always plenty of work to be done at the end of each
day's flying. Both of the engines had to be overhauled and cleaned,
all parts of the machine examined and petrol and oil tanks refilled
for the next journey. Usually this took us three or four hours
every day. We adopted a set program which we always carried out
religiously. As soon as the machine landed Bennett and Shiers would
don their overalls and set to work on the engines; the sparking plugs
would be taken out and cleaned, magnetos examined and all parts
of the engine inspected and cleaned. On this work to a large extent
depended our success or failure.

Keith and I would climb out of our seats and talk to the people who had come out to meet us. Presently Keith would make enquiries about our petrol and oil supplies and get them brought up to the Vimy. I would then go off to the nearest post office and send our cables and get back to the Vimy as soon as I could. In addition, we had to run the gauntlet of functions and ceremonies, and it was difficult to make folk understand that work had to be done. We deeply appreciated every one's generous kindness, but I fear that on some occasions people must have thought us very discourteous.

By the time I returned to the machine Keith would have the petrol ready to put into the tanks and we would start to work. This was very tiring and monotonous. I would open the four-gallon cans and lift them up to my brother, a distance of about six feet, and he would empty the cans into the tanks through a large funnel with a chamois leather strainer. Usually we lifted and filtered about half a ton of petrol into the machine and sometimes as much as a ton if we had just completed a long flight. I have always regarded this work as the hardest part of the whole flight. We would land more or less tired after several hours in the air and then start on really hard work again. The temptation was always to let some one else do it and go off ourselves and rest, but other people might not have filtered the petrol properly, or done something wrong. We decided before we started that we would do *all* the work on the machine ourselves and as far as possible we carried this out.

By the time the tanks were full Bennett and Shiers would have the engines finished; we would then fill up the oil tanks with Castrol, put the covers over the cockpit, and peg the machine down for the night.

Putting in the Castrol was always a messy job and we would usually finish our day's work very tired and very oily.

Fortunately we had foreseen all this and talked about it before we started; each man knew exactly what he had to do, and did it, and I think that any one who has studied human nature will agree that, under these conditions, it is a remarkable fact that never once was there a misunderstanding or a cross word spoken amongst our four selves.

On many occasions it was 9 or 10 pm before we left the machine for the night; we would then go off to either a hotel or some kind friend's house, bathe, dine, and in due course—to bed. Each day we arose at 4.30 am and we never once had more than five hours' sleep a night, usually it was about four, and then on through another similar day. Add to this the thrill, excitement, and strain of the whole race against time and one realises that it is fortunate that we had gone into training and got ourselves very fit before leaving England.

On the morning of November 23rd we made a daylight start from Basra for Bundar Abbas,[3] 630 miles southeast. Soon after starting, the sun came up from the distant hills; the world threw off its sombre grey, and in dawn's fair raiment became beautiful. The delicate shades of pink that flushed the horizon mounted higher and higher until the zenith grew gay; and so another day of the flight had begun.

The sunlight sparkled on our varnished wings, and the polished propellers became halos of shimmering light. Our engines sang away merrily. The Vimy ceased to be a machine and pulsed with life, as if feeling the glory of the morning; my brother scanned the landscape below, plotting off the course on the chart and checking our position from time to time by villages and salient features,

3   Or Bandar Abbas, a port city on the Persian Gulf.

remarking how wonderfully accurate the world was created!

Bennett and Shiers had stowed themselves away in the after cockpit and were reclining inside the fuselage with the spare parts, endeavouring to secure well-earned rest from their strenuous efforts of the past few days. As the spare parts crammed all available space, theirs was painful comfort indeed. The dimensions of our front cockpit were of those adequate proportions generally attributed to wedges. The weather continued fine, but for the most part the flight was uninteresting and monotonous.

We passed over Bushire[4] and several coastal villages, but the only really impressive sight was the ruggedness of the coastal belt and the hinterland ridges. Some of the country presents a remarkable sight, and appears as if a mighty harrow had torn down the mountain sides into abysmal furrows. Fantastic-shaped ridges and razor-backs rise precipitously from deep valleys, barren of vegetation and desolate of life. Occasionally we passed over small flat plains dotted with abrupt hills and flat tabletops. The whole earth appeared as though some terrific convulsion had swept it and left in its wake this fantastic chaos of scarred mountains and gouged valleys.

In striking contrast, the shores of this wild scene are washed by the stagnant waters of the Persian Gulf. The colouration of this phenomenal panorama was equally bewildering. The dead expanse of the Persian Gulf, mingled with the mud of the rivers, was an exquisite shade of green, patched here and there with darker areas, where the wind had caught it up into ripples.

Mountainward, the first impression was that all had been moulded in yellow clay. A closer survey showed streakings and strata of infinite shades, of which the rust colour of ironstone appeared

---

4   Bushire or Bushehr is a seaport on the Persian Gulf coast of south-western Iran.

dominant. At intervals the dry beds of waterways cut well-marked defiles from the high mountains to the sea. They stood out like roadways winding through the maze and seeming as if blasted out by the hand of man.

Throughout this terrible country I scarcely observed a possible landing ground, and had our engines failed us it would have meant either crashing or else an immersion in the Persian Gulf. So it was with no small relief that I brought the Vimy to a safe landing at Bundar Abbas, where a hearty welcome was extended to us by the British Consul, the Persian Governor, and a great concourse of interested natives.

Although dog-tired, I could not sleep much that night. The coming day's trip, I hoped, would enable us to reach Karachi in a non-stop flight of 730 miles. The distance did not perturb me in the least, but the treacherous country and the isolation from civilization in case of a forced landing, and another long stretch of detestable mountain-scored country, was in itself enough to give one a nightmare.

The British Consul had prepared an ostentatious-looking document which we were to carry. It commanded the murderous tribes which infested the country to treat us kindly, in case we were compelled to land among them!

Fortune favoured us once more with a following breeze and excellent weather. The country was a repetition of that passed over the previous day, and, with the morning sunlight striking aslant, heavy shadows gave the scene the semblance of a mighty rasp.

The engines were perfectly synchronized, and roared away harmoniously; but it is imperative for the pilot to watch every part of his machine, especially the engines. As I sat there hour after hour, I found myself automatically performing the same cycle of observation over and over again.

My supreme difficulty was to keep my sleep-heavy eyelids from closing and my head from nodding. First of all I would look at my starboard engine and see that the oil-pressure gauge and revolution counter were registering correctly; then listen to hear if the engine was firing evenly. Next, glance over the engine and oil-pipe connections and check off the thermometer which indicated the water temperature in the radiators. The altimeter, airspeed indicator, and petrol-flow indicator in turn claimed attention.

I would then look up to the port engine and go over the instruments and engine as before; then over the side to scan the landscape, and ever keep an alert eye for a suitable spot in case of a forced landing.

By the time I had completed this performance it would be time to start all over again. When flying over interesting country the monotony of this ceaseless routine is relieved, but when flying over country such as the present stage the only mental stimulus that buoyed us up was the anticipation of rosier times ahead. Often our thoughts were of Poulet, who was somewhere ahead, and we wondered if ever we would catch up with him.

Frequently we passed over small villages, and our advent instilled terror into the inhabitants and their animals.

For the last 100 miles we left the coast and flew on a compass bearing direct for Karachi and so we entered the aerial gateway to India after a non-stop flight of eight and a half hours.

CHAPTER VII

Karachi to Rangoon

T he usual procedure of overhauling the engines and machine and refilling our tanks with petrol had to be carried out before we could seek rest, but the first news that greeted us on landing at Karachi was gratifying. Poulet was at Delhi, only a day's flight in the lead! This was a great surprise, for we fully expected that he would be well on his way to Singapore. From now onward added zest would be given to the flight, for I intended to pursue the chase in keen earnest. Already I considered the race as good as won, for the Vimy was superior both in speed and range.

We had hoped for a good rest at Karachi, but the local Royal Air Force officers had arranged a dinner, and it was not before 'the very witching hour' that we turned to bed. Three hours and a half later we were called to continue the flight. This was to be one of the longest non-stops we had undertaken. Nine hours' flying should land us in Delhi, 720 miles away.

After circling above the aerodrome we turned east, heading straight into the golden sun that was just rising above the horizon. A low ground haze that changed into a golden mist as the sun mounted higher hid the earth from view. Passing over Hyderabad, the vapours rolled away and we had a grand view of the River Indus. Once more we entered the monotony of the desert. For the next three hours we flew steadily onward, pursuing the railroad track across the dreary Sind Desert.

It was a joy to reach Ajmere,[1] a delightful little city, beautifully situated in a basin of green hills. The country beyond is for the most part flat—a vast verdant carpet irrigated from the great rivers. Practically from the time we had reached the African coast, when on our way to Cairo, the flight had been across deserts or desolate lands. Now the new prospect that opened ahead invited and attracted.

During the afternoon flying conditions became very boisterous, and the turbulent atmosphere tossed the Vimy about like a small vessel in a heavy sea. This I also accepted as a welcome diversion, for the flights of the past few days had cramped me in one position, and now I was kept actively on the move keeping the machine straight and fighting the air-pockets and bumps into which we plunged and fell.

We first noticed Delhi from fifty miles distance—a white streak in a haziness of green plain. Quickly details became apparent, and soon the streak had germinated into a considerable town.

I circled above Delhi to allow the people to see our machine, which had established a record by arriving thirteen days after leaving London—a distance of 5,790 miles. We climbed crampily out of the machine and were welcomed by General McEwan, the Royal Air Force chief in India, and many other old friends.

I regretted that I was quite unable to reply to their kindly expressions, as I did not hear them. The roar of the exhausts for nine consecutive hours' flying had affected my ears so that I was quite deaf.

---

1   Ajmer is a city in the Indian state of Rajasthan.

After several hours my hearing returned, and it was to learn that Poulet had left the same morning for Allahabad.[2] Great excitement prevailed, for one aeroplane had departed and another had arrived on the same day, both engaged in a race halfway around the world! After attending to the machine we dined at the RAF mess, thoroughly tired but extremely happy. Half the journey was completed and Poulet was within range.

We had left Basra at 6 am on November 23rd and arrived at Delhi fifty-six hours later, covering a distance of 2,100 miles. Out of the fifty-six hours we had spent twenty-five hours ten minutes actually in the air, and in the balance we had over-hauled the engines and machine twice, and had by our own efforts lifted and filtered two and three-quarter tons of petrol into the machine.

I had intended pushing on to Allahabad next day, but on arrival at the aerodrome we were feeling the effects of the past strenuous days so severely that I decided a rest was imperative. We took it in the form of the proverbial change of work—and, putting in six good hours on the machine, made everything ready for an early morrow start. Toward evening my brother and I drove into the city, sight-seeing.

As I had been to Delhi during my flight to Calcutta with General Borton, I played the guide, and an enjoyable ramble through this future capital diverted our thoughts from the Vimy for the moment and enabled us to relax.

Further diversion, with less relaxation, was provided by the native driver of a car we hired. In the language of the realm in which we had been living, he navigated full out and nearly crashed us on several occasions, in his desire to show what a pilot he was. I declare that I 'had the wind up' far more often on this bit of journey than

2   Now known officially as Prayagraj.

Aerial view of the Taj Mahal in the city of Agra, India, November,
taken from the Vimy during the race. [Ross and Keith Smith Collection,
SLSA PRG 18/9/1/20C]

during the whole flight. However, the casualties were few and the fatalities nil, and we paid him off at the RAF quarters.

At 4.30 next morning I tumbled stiffly out of bed on the insistence of a Yankee alarm-clock. Oh, for another day off! But by the time the others had uncoiled and emerged into the early Indian dawn, I felt again the keenness of the chase. A friendly RAF pilot came up in a Bristol Fighter and flew with us for a few miles along the course of the Jumna.[3]

Half an hour later the oil-gauge surprised us by setting back to zero, and we made an unexpected landing at Muttra,[4] to find that it was happily only a minor trouble—the slipping of the indicator on its spindle. And so into the air once more, and on to Agra—Agra the city of the Taj Mahal.

Of all the remembered scenes, wonderful and beautiful, that of the Taj Mahal remains the most vivid and the most exquisite. There it lay below us, dazzling in the strong sunlight—a vision in marble. Seen from the ground, one's emotions are stirred by the extraordinary delicacy of its workmanship. Viewed from 3,000 feet above, the greater part of its infinite detail is lost, but one sees it as a whole. It lies like a perfectly executed miniature, or a matchless white jewel reclining in a setting of Nature's emeralds.

We hovered lazily around, exposed our photographic plates, and swung off on our course. In the vastness of space through which we were speeding, the magnificent monument became a toy ... a mote ... a memory. New scenes, villages, and towns rose from the unreachable brink ahead, grew into being, passed beneath, then out over the brim of the world behind us.

---

3   A river in northern India with its source in the Himalayas.
4   Mathura, in the state of Uttar Pradesh.

We were crossing the vast plains of Central India, a great flat tessellation of cultivated patches that gave an impression of the earth being covered with green, brown, and golden tiles. These multi-tinted patches were framed with brimming channels carrying the irrigation waters from the great river. Allahabad was reached after four and a half hours, and we eagerly but vainly searched the aerodrome for a glimpse of Poulet. There were several hangars on the aerodrome, however, and we thought that his machine might be under cover, but on landing we were informed that he had left that same morning for Calcutta.

It was too late to continue the chase that afternoon, but next morning saw us early on the wing.

Once more pursuing the course of the Jumna as far as Benares,[5] we headed southeast and followed the railroad to Calcutta. Forty miles north of Calcutta we came above the River Hooghly.[6]

Here and there factories and jute mills came into view, with villages clustering around them. The villages grew dense and became the outskirts of a great and expansive city—a mighty congestion of buildings, white, glaring in the sun; green patches and gardens, thoroughfares teeming with people, a vast fleet of shipping, of docks and activities and Calcutta slipped away beneath us.

Thousands of people had collected on the racecourse, at the far side of the city, to witness our arrival, and when we landed it was with great difficulty that the police kept back the multitude of natives that surged around the machine. A barrier was at last placed around the Vimy, and soon we became the centre of a compact mass

5   Also known as Varanasi.

6   Also the Bhāgirathi-Hooghly, and traditionally called 'Ganga', the river is a tributary of the Ganges River in West Bengal.

Vickers Vimy landing at Calcutta, India, 28 November 1919.
[Ross and Keith Smith Collection, SLSA PRG 18/7/14]

of peering faces, all struggling to get closer and obtain a better view. The elusive Poulet, we learned, had moved off the same morning for Akyab.[7]

That night, after the usual overhaul of engines and filling up with petrol, we stayed with friends and slept well. We had crossed India and were now more than half-way to Australia.

Our departure next morning from Calcutta was marked by an incident that to the layman may sound insignificant, but it might easily have spelled disaster to us. Thousands of natives and a great many distinguished white people came down to see the start. The race-course is really too small for a machine as large as our Vimy to manoeuvre with safety, and I was a trifle nervous about the take-off; but the surface was good, our engines in fine trim, and she rose like a bird.

Then came our narrow escape. A large number of kite hawks were flying around, alarmed by the size and noise of this new great

---

7   Today's Sittwe, capital of Rakhine State in Myanmar.

bird in their midst. When we had cleared the ground by about ten feet two hawks flew across us at an angle; they seemed to become confused and turned straight into us, one striking the wing and the other flying straight into the port propeller. There was a crash as if a stone had hit the blade, and then a scatter of feathers.

It may not sound very dreadful—except for the hawk—but as a matter of fact it was a breathless, not to say a terrifying moment, for we fully expected to hear the crash of broken propeller blades.

We were at the time flying straight for the high trees, and, had the propeller broken, nothing could have saved us from a terrible crash. However, more hawks were circling about, and in endeavouring to avoid them I almost crashed the machine on the tree-tops. By a very narrow margin indeed we cleared them, and I was deeply relieved when we had climbed to 1,000 feet and were clear of the pestilent birds. I marvelled that our propeller stood the impact, for a very trifling knock will cause the disruption of a propeller when running 'full out', and so in an extremely high state of tension. (I have known so tiny an object as a cigarette end thrown carelessly into a propeller to cause the whirling blades to fly to pieces!)

On looking over the machine I noticed one of the hawk's wings had become pinned in the rigging, and we secured it after the day's flight as a souvenir of a hairbreadth escape.

Calcutta marked the completion of the second stage of our journey, and from now onward the route would be much more difficult and hazardous. We had had the benefit of RAF aerodromes and personnel at almost every landing place, but henceforth we would have to land on race-courses, or very small aerodromes. Also, I knew that the only possible landing places right on to Port Darwin were at stated places hundreds of miles apart, and that in the event of engine trouble our chances of making a safe forced landing were very slender.

I had originally intended flying from Calcutta to Rangoon[8] race-course in one flight, but as the next day, November 29th, was a Saturday, and I was informed that a race meeting would be held at Rangoon on that day, I decided to stop at Akyab.

We were now passing above a dreaded span of country, the Sundarbans,[9] where engine trouble would have meant the undoing of all our efforts and labour. The mouth of the Ganges here frays out into a network of streams, producing a jigsaw of innumerable islets and swamps. We breathed much more freely after we had reached Chittagong,[10] a place I had reason to remember well, through having spent four days there the previous year, when our ship caught fire and was blown up.

From Chittagong we followed the coast-line of Burma, and eventually reached Akyab. My brother peered over the side as we circled above the aerodrome and showed symptoms of great excitement, while Bennett and Shiers waved joyfully from their cockpit and pointed down to the ground. They indicated a small machine near the centre of the field. It was Poulet!

Poulet was the first to greet us on landing. He came forward with a cheery smile and outstretched hand—a true sportsman, the hero of a gallant and daring enterprise. I was deeply interested in inspecting Poulet's machine, which was drawn up alongside the Vimy. In proportion the contrast was reminiscent of an eagle and a sparrow. The Vimy towered above the tiny Caudron, which appeared

---

8   Today's Yangon.

9   The Sundarbans, meaning 'beautiful forest', is a coastal mangrove area stretching from the Hooghly River to the Baleswar in modern day Bangladesh.

10 Now officially Chattogram and a major coastal city in Bangladesh.

altogether too frail and quite unsuited for the hazardous task these two courageous fellows had embarked upon. I had a long talk with Poulet and his mechanic, Benoist; they made fun of their adventures and intimated that theirs was a novel and exciting method of touring the globe.

We agreed to fly on together the next day to Rangoon, but when morning arrived, as we still had some work to complete on the machine, Poulet set off, and by the time we were ready he had an hour's lead. No aeroplane had ever landed at Rangoon before, and naturally I was very keen to win the honour for the Vimy. For the first 100 miles I followed the coast-line southward and did not observe a single landing place in case of necessity. The coast, for the most part, fringes out into vast mangrove swamps, while further inland the country becomes mountainous, with rice-fields checkering the valleys and every available irrigable area. The hills are densely wooded and very rugged.

Flying east, we crossed a low mountain chain, and on the other side found the Irrawaddy River.[11] I followed down its course as far as Prome.[12] From here the railroad guided us on to Rangoon. I had no difficulty in locating the landing ground the race-course, a green patch framed by a compact ring of cheering humanity.

We came to earth midst tempestuous cheering, and were welcomed by the Lieutenant-Governor of Burma, Sir Reginald Craddock and Lady Craddock. We were told that no race meeting had been so well attended as the present, nor had the betting been so widespread. The multitudes had massed to witness two aeroplanes racing half-way across the globe. To them the race was more than

---

11 Now officially the Ayeyarwady River.

12 Pyay.

Arrival of Vickers Vimy at Burma [Ross and Keith Smith Collection,
SLSA PRG 18/9/1/30D]

novel; it was a great event in their lives, for few indeed of the vast
assemblage had ever seen an aeroplane.

As flying conditions from Akyab had been boisterous, we in our
high-powered machine had a great advantage over Poulet, and in
spite of the hour's handicap at the outset, we succeeded in reaching
Rangoon an hour ahead of him. Poulet's arrival was the signal for
another outburst of cheering, and he was welcomed no less warmly
than ourselves.

The police experienced great difficulty in clearing the race-
course that evening, as many of the natives had brought their food
and beds, intent on holding a festival for the duration of our stay.
I was told that when the first news of our departure from London
appeared in the local papers, and the fact that we intended calling
at Rangoon became known, a large crowd of natives straightway
assembled on the race-course, expecting to see us arrive in a few

The Vimy surrounded by a crowd at Rangoon, 30 November.
[Ross and Keith Smith Collection, SLSA PRG 18/16/14]

hours. Later, when the news of our reaching Akyab was noised abroad, a multitude camped overnight on the race-course, so as to make sure of witnessing our arrival.

That night we were the guests of Sir Reginald and Lady Craddock, who did everything possible for our comfort and insisted that we should go to bed early. It was the first time such a suggestion had been made to us, and, as we were very weary, we deeply appreciated their kindly consideration.

There is a strange lizard in the East which makes a peculiar noise, like 'tuk-too', and it is a popular superstition that if one hears this sound repeated seven times, good luck will follow. That night, just before going to our rooms, a lizard 'tuk-tood' seven times. The omen was good and we slept peacefully.

CHAPTER VIII

In the Clouds above Burma

We had arranged with Poulet to start off together next morning and keep company as far as Bangkok. The Vimy was considerably faster than the Caudron, but by throttling down and manoeuvring, it would be possible to keep together. The way to Bangkok lay across high ranges and dense jungle, and the mutual advantage in making the journey together over this unfrequented and practically unknown country, should a forced landing have to be made by one of us, was obvious.

Traffic fills the highways before sunrise in the East, and a considerable portion of it was moving toward the race-course. A great crowd of interested natives swarmed over the aerodrome, and the police and troops were already busily engaged clearing them off prior to our departure. We started up the engines, took leave of our kind friends, and waited for Poulet. Poulet had some difficulty with his machine; and as it was a warm morning and our engines were beginning to get hot, I took off intending to circle above the aerodrome until Poulet arose on the wing.

The take-off was not without a thrill. As a matter of fact, to this day it is a mystery to me that we ever left the ground. The race-course was much too small for so large a machine as the Vimy and heavily laden as it was. It had barely attained flying speed when a fence loomed up in front of us. The Vimy just scraped over, but ahead were trees and buildings. I acted instinctively. The undercarriage brushed the tree-top, and danger was past. It was over in a breathless moment; but had the machine been but a single foot lower, disaster must have overtaken us. How slender is the cord that holds success from failure!

I circled above the race-course for twenty minutes; but, as Poulet had not yet left the ground, I concluded that he must be experiencing engine trouble, and so reluctantly we had to push off without him.

We flew due east to Moulmein,[1] immortalized in Kipling's famous ballad, 'On the Road to Mandalay', and as no aeroplane had ever flown above this land before, Sergeant Shiers, in words worthy of the great poet, said it was fine to be flitting through air that had never smelt a blanky exhaust!

The maps we carried of this country were very poor and sadly lacking in detail, but they indicated that a 7,000-foot mountain range had to be crossed before reaching Bangkok.

After leaving Moulmein we headed southeast over country rapidly becoming mountainous; but, instead of encountering lofty summits, a mighty cloud bank, that seemed to reach to heaven and bar the entire prospect in the direction of our course, extended before us. The monsoon season was now due, and I concluded that this would be one of the initial storms. Somewhere in that dread barrier lay the high peaks over which we must cross, and I admit that I was afraid of the prospect. As time wore on, the storms would grow in frequency and intensity, so I decided to plunge ahead.

The clouds rested down to 4,000 feet, and we were flying just beneath them. Somewhere ahead lay the mountains that had to be

---

1   Now Mawlamyine or Mawlamyaing.

crossed, rearing their summits another 3,000 feet higher. Our maps indicated a pass which we tried to find, and so we started off along a deep valley. At first it looked hopeful, but after five minutes' flying the cliffs narrowed in, and, fearing I might be trapped in a tapering dead end, I turned the Vimy about. There was just sufficient room in which to effect the manoeuvre.

After a consultation with my brother, we agreed that our safest course was to climb above the cloud-mass or at least to an altitude sufficiently high to clear the mountain tops, and barge our way through the mist. At 9,000 feet we emerged above the first layer; but eastward the clouds appeared to terrace up gradually, and in the distance there extended still another great wall, towering several thousand feet higher.

Before starting off over this sea of clouds, my brother took observations with the drift indicator, and we found to our dismay that we would have to fight into a twenty-mile-an-hour head wind. He gave me the compass bearing to fly on, and away we went once more, with the world lost to view beneath us. It reminded me of our first day over France; but the weather was not so cold, so we felt physically more comfortable. The map showed the range to be about fifty miles wide, and after we had flown for half an hour, still another cloud barrier appeared directly ahead.

Our machine had now reached its 'ceiling', so there was no alternative but to plunge ahead into the mist. We were then flying at an altitude of 11,000 feet, and were soon engulfed in a dense blanket of mist. As we had left England hurriedly, there had been no time to fit special cloud-navigating instruments, and the only ones we carried for this purpose were the ordinary compass, air-speed indicator, and inclinometer. Any one who has flown through clouds in a big machine, under similar circumstances, will appreciate my feelings at this time.

Down below us lay jagged mountain peaks buried by cloud. Ahead, around, and behind, the mist enfolded us in an impenetrable screen, and if I once allowed the machine to get beyond control, a horrible fate would be waiting for us all below.

To those who have not experienced the anxiety of cloud-flying, I will attempt to describe briefly what happens.

The moment one plunges into heavy cloud there is misty blankness; all objects are lost to view; and as time wears on, a helpless feeling grows upon one that all sense of direction is lost. To overcome this predicament, I was provided with the aforementioned instruments, and settled down to try to watch all three at once and maintain their readings correctly. In addition it was necessary to glance over the engines and the gauges continually.

At first all went well; but, while turning to check over an engine, I apparently and unconsciously, with the natural movement of my body, pushed one foot, which was on the rudder bar, slightly forward. This turned the machine off its course, and when I next looked at my compass I was ten degrees off course. I then kicked on the opposite rudder to bring the machine back; but as the Vimy is much more sensitive to respond than the comparatively sluggish compass-needle, I found that I had put on too much rudder. The result was that when the compass-needle started to swing, it did so through an angle of forty-five degrees.

In my attempt to correct the course and bring the needle back on to its correct reading, I glanced at the air-speed indicator and found it registering over one hundred miles an hour—twenty-five miles above normal flying speed. This meant that I must have pushed the nose of the machine down. The inclinometer indicated that the machine was not flying laterally correct; in fact, we were flying at an inclined angle of thirty degrees.

I realised that the machine was slipping sideways, and that if I did not get matters righted at once, the machine would get out of control and go spinning down to earth.

It is useless attempting to describe how I acted. A pilot does things instinctively, and presently my instruments told me that we were once more on our course and on an even keel.

All this took but a few seconds; but they were anxious moments, as a single mistake or the losing of one's head would have been fatal. This happened several times, and at the end of what seemed hours I glanced at my watch and found we had only been in the clouds for twelve minutes! Perhaps my nerves were a little ragged, owing to strain and lack of sleep during the past fortnight; but I felt at last that anything would be better than going on under these tense and nerve-racking conditions.

It was now an hour since we first started across the clouds, and both Keith and I concluded that we must surely be across the mountain range. So I decided to take the risk and go lower and 'feel'.

Shutting off both engines, we glided down, and I held up the machine so that we were going as slowly as possible—only about forty miles an hour.

The sensation was akin to the captain navigating a vessel in uncharted shoaling seas—expecting every moment to feel a bump. Lower and lower we went—ten, nine, eight thousand feet—and then we both anxiously peered over the sides—straining for a glimpse of hidden peaks.

As we approached the 7,000-foot level, which I knew to be the height of the range, we huddled together and held on tight, in anticipation of the crash! I noticed a small hole in the cloud, with something dark beneath. It was past in a flash, but instantly I pulled the throttle full open and flew level again. At first I thought it was the top of a dreadful peak, but on further consideration I remembered that in my brief glance the dark patch had looked a long way down.

Once more I shut off and went lower, and as we had not hit anything by the time we reached 4,000 feet, I concluded that the range had been crossed.

A few minutes more and we burst out into full view of a glorious world, carpeted with trees, 1,500 feet below. The sudden transformation was stunning. It was an unspeakable relief—the end of an hour that was one of the veriest nightmare experiences I have ever passed through.

Before our bewildered gaze there stretched a dark-green forest, only limited by the distant skyline. Here and there the dark green was splashed with patches of bright-coloured creeper, and in spite of the fact that there was not the vestige of a possible landing place, it was beautiful and a welcome relief. Later, the Siamese told us that all this country was unexplored.

The country now began to fall away gradually to the east; the hills became less rugged and petered out into undulating, yet heavily wooded, jungle. An hour later and we reached the Mekon River[2] and the haunts of man. Small villages lay scattered along its banks and wide expanses of irrigated lands verdant with rice crops.

Following downstream, we landed at Don Muang aerodrome,[3]

2   Mekong.
3   Don Mueang, today one of the two international airports serving Bangkok.

twelve miles north of Bangkok, after a flight that will live long in my memory. Don Muang is the headquarters of the Siamese Flying Corps. They have several hangars, a number of machines, and up-to-date workshops. During my visit to Siam the previous year I had been to Don Muang, so that on landing I found myself among friends. We were met by the British Consul General, Mr T.H. Lyle, with whom I had stayed on my previous visit and who now rendered us valuable and appreciated assistance.

The Siamese also displayed the warmest hospitality, and the Commandant very kindly placed his own bungalow at our disposal. It was found necessary to regrind the valves on two of the cylinders of the starboard engine; and, as this was a lengthy job, Bennett and Shiers worked all night to complete it, so that we might keep to our usual scheduled starting time. An electric lamp was rigged up over the engine, and all the flying ants and insects in Siam collected around it, which greatly added to the discomfort and hindrance of the work.

My original plan was to fly from Bangkok to Singapore, roughly 1,000 miles, in one flight; but as I learned there was a good aerodrome at Singora,[4] about half-way, with 500 gallons of petrol depôted there, and as I was anxious to conserve the machine as much as possible, I decided to land at the latter place.

---

4   Nowadays Songkhla, a port city in Southern Thailand.

CHAPTER IX

Siam to Singapore

We left Bangkok in good weather, and were escorted for the first fifty miles by four Siamese machines. For the first hour the flying conditions were ideal, with a good following wind helping us; then ahead again lay our old enemies, the clouds. At this time we were flying along the coast, so did not deem it necessary to climb above them. The clouds became lower and heavier and soon we found ourselves only 1,000 feet above the sea.

Ahead we saw the rain, and I dreaded what was to come. While we were over the sea, with the land on our right, there was comparatively little chance of our crashing into anything. This was fortunate, for in a few moments we were soaked through, our goggles became saturated, and all vision for more than a few hundred yards or so was obliterated. The rain came down literally like a sheet of water, and as we had to remove our goggles and maintain a constant lookout ahead, we were almost blinded by the rain lashing our unprotected eyes.

At this time we were doing ninety miles per hour, and as the torrential rain dashed against us and the machine it pattered and smote like hail. Narrowing my eyes down to slits, I peered out ahead as long as I could endure it; that was but a few minutes. I then tapped Keith to keep the watch while I rested my eyes; then, when he could see no more, I would 'carry on' again. So it went on for the best part of three hours. Fortunately this heavy rain was not continuous, but the squalls which we went through at frequent intervals generally took ten minutes to pass.

Still another difficulty presented itself. As long as we were flying south, the strong wind helped us; but as we had to follow the coast-line in detail, and there were many bays and headlands, we frequently found ourselves fighting right into the teeth of the gale to get out of a bay or weather a headland.

I was afraid to go inland, as the rain only allowed us limited visibility. Once we almost crashed on to a hill, which suddenly loomed up through the rain ahead. I just had time, by a hair's breadth, to pull the machine around in a climbing turn and go farther out to sea. I have never experienced worse flying conditions, and had it been at all possible to land, I gladly would have done so.

All the flat stretches along the coast were paddy fields under water. We were wet and miserable, and the thought oftentimes came over me of what an ignominious end it would be if we had engine trouble and were forced to land in a paddy-field of mud and water. I wondered at our marvellous engines—through the snows of France, the blaze of the tropics, and through these terrible rains, they still roared merrily on.

An hour before reaching Singora we passed through and outstripped the storm. As the clouds were still low, we kept our altitude down to 1,000 feet, passing here and there scattered villages, scaring the water buffaloes, which would career off, flashing across the paddy-fields as fast as their bulk would allow.

At last we reached Singora, and a glance at the aerodrome showed that at least half of it was under water. There was, however, a narrow

Crowds gathered to view the Vimy at Singora, Thailand, December.
[Ross and Keith Smith Collection, SLSA PRG 18/7/20]

strip along the centre which appeared more or less dry, but I would have to make a landing across wind. I came down low to examine this strip, and to my utter dismay noticed that it was covered with small tree-stumps!

A wide and anxious circling around the aerodrome showed me there was no other spot on which to land; so there was nothing for it but to attempt to make a landing on this narrow strip of stump-studded ground.

As we touched and ran along, I expected every moment to feel a jolt and the under-carriage wrenched off, or else the machine thrown on to her nose; but by the merciful guidance of Providence we miraculously came to rest safely.

The only damage sustained was to our tail-skid, which had caught in a stump and been wrenched off. I walked back along our tracks and found that in several instances our wheels had missed by a few inches stumps a foot to eighteen inches high.

The whole native population assembled to see us. None had ever seen an aeroplane before, and at first they would not venture near. There were three Englishmen at Singora, and one of them had imposed upon the simple native minds that the devil was going to arrive in a flying chariot to take charge over all the convicts there. When, however, they saw that four ordinary humans climbed out of the machine, they quickly surged around us. I noticed that they were staring, arguing, and pointing at us in a peculiar way; but it was not until I heard of our friend's joke that I understood the full significance of their interest in us.

Several of them walked in front of the machine, flapping their arms and performing birdlike evolutions. We concluded that they were solving the mystery of flight and demonstrating how the Vimy flapped its wings to rise from the ground. My brother, unobserved, climbed into the cockpit and, seizing the control column, vigorously moved it to and fro, which caused the ailerons[1] and elevators to flap about.

There was a wild scamper in all directions. We learned afterward that the natives imagined that we were flapping our wings preparatory to starting off.

My first inquiry was as to the quantity of petrol available. I discovered that the supposed 500 gallons was only 500 litres, depôted there for Poulet. This meant we would be compelled to remain here

---

[1] Hinged portions on the end of the wings used for banking when turning. [Original footnote]

until I could get sufficient petrol from Penang or Bangkok to take us on to Singapore. I accordingly sent off an urgent wire to the Asiatic Petroleum Company at Penang, asking them to send me 200 gallons of aviation petrol as speedily as possible.

I also wired the Resident Councillor at Penang, asking him to assist in the event of there being difficulty in getting this quantity of petrol shipped at such short notice. I next requested the Governor of Singora to have part of the aerodrome cleared of stumps to enable us to take off.

Our machine was left standing on the strip of high ground and we pegged her down securely for the night.

Our next contract was to mend the tail-skid. An examination showed that the fitting which attaches it to the fuselage had been broken off. This meant at least six hours' work, provided we could find the necessary materials. One of our English friends took us to a local Chinaman, a jack of all trades and the master of a promising heap of scrap-iron. Bennett unearthed a piece of steel shafting which, provided a lathe was available to turn it down to shape and size, fitted our purpose.

We then proceeded to a near-by rice mill which was just whistling off for the night. There we found a good lathe, but of primitive motive power. Four coolies turned a large pulley-wheel, and their power was transmitted by belt to the lathe.

Bennett got to work at once by the light of a kerosene lamp. After an hour's hard work, little impression was made on the steel, and our four coolie-power engine 'konked out'.

Four more coolies were secured, but after half an hour they went on strike and demanded more money. I gave them the increase, but fifteen minutes later they went on strike again. This time we called the foreman from the rice mill. There was a different kind of strike, and so the work proceeded.

By 10 pm Bennett had completed the job, and, considering the makeshift tools, it was a remarkably fine piece of workmanship and skill.

Rain began to fall, so we returned to the bungalow which had been placed at our disposal by HRH Prince Yugula.[2]

Just before midnight we were awakened by the sound of a torrential downpour—the storm which we had passed through during the day had reached Singora. The wind increased to a gale, and, fearing that the machine might be in danger, we all turned out and kept watch. Fortunately, we had pegged her nose into the wind, but during the heavy squalls the Vimy so strained at her lashings that several times I feared she would be swept away and crashed.

We stood by all night, obtaining what little shelter we could from the wings, and at every squall rushed out and held on to the planes. Needless to say, we were drenched to the skin, and when the wind eased down shortly after daybreak, we felt tired and miserable, with no dry clothes to put on.

Ten inches of rain had fallen during the night, and the whole of the aerodrome, excepting the ridge on which the machine was standing, resembled a lake. Luckily, the ground was sandy, and after the rain ceased the water drained off rapidly. Squalls continued throughout the day, but Bennett and Shiers, after rigging a tarpaulin shelter, were able to work on their engines.

After breakfast in the bungalow we returned to the machine and found that the government had sent down 200 convicts from the local

---

2   Yugala Dighambara, Prince of Lopburi, was the Cambridge-educated son of King
     Chulalongkorn of Siam.

jail to clear away the stumps; and so we set them to work to clear a strip about 400 yards long and fifty yards wide across the aerodrome.

The day's rest from flying was a delightful relaxation; in fact, an imperative necessity, for my brother's and my own eyes were almost too painful for vision, after the previous day's battle with the storm.

Late that afternoon our petrol arrived from Penang, but it was raining too heavily to risk putting it into the machine. We were greatly indebted to Captain Owen Hughes, an ex-Royal Air Force officer, for bringing up the petrol and also for his prompt attention in arranging for its transport.

After a much-needed night's rest, we were down at the aerodrome at daylight, and after putting the 200 gallons of petrol into the tanks, started up the engines. Getting the machine into the air was a questionable problem, but, as our time for reaching Australia was fast closing in, we decided to make the attempt.

Three large patches of water extended across the aerodrome at intervals of about fifty yards. This water was, on the average, six inches deep; but, as the aerodrome was sandy, our wheels did not sink appreciably into it. A clear run of fifty yards allowed the machine to gather a fair headway. Then she struck the water, which almost pulled us up; a race across another fifty yards of hard ground, and by the time we had passed through the second patch of water the machine was moving very little faster than at the beginning.

The third patch of ground was a little longer, and when we reached the third pool we were travelling at about thirty miles per hour.

The sudden impact with the water almost threw the Vimy on to her nose, and water was sucked up and whirled in every direction by the propellers.

Our flying speed had to be gained on the seventy yards of dry ground which now remained; beyond that extended scrub and gorse bushes.

The Vimy bounded forward as soon as she left the water, and just managed to get sufficient lift on her wings to clear a ditch and scrape over the shrub.

I had been informed that the weather would be much better on the western coast of the peninsula, so we followed the railway line across to that side. As the clouds hung only a few hundred feet above the railroad, we were compelled to descend to a perilously low altitude, which was rendered the more hazardous by huge limestone outcrops, rising four to five hundred feet, scattered over the country.

Along the western shores we found the weather much improved; the clouds were higher, and occasional bursts of sunshine threw weird light and shadow effects across the paddy-fields and scattered villages. We still maintained a low altitude, which added greatly to the interest of the flight and also gave us a splendid opportunity of studying intimately this remarkable and productive country.

Near Kaular Lumpar[3] we entered the tin mining country and observed many dredges in full operation. Lower still we flew across the rubber plantations, cheered by the planters and waving back. Then, passing above Malacca, we reached Singapore in the afternoon, after one of the most interesting stages of the journey.

I had been dreading the landing and take-off at Singapore, as the improvised aerodrome, the racecourse, was altogether too small for our large machine.

I glided the Vimy down at as low a speed as possible, and just before we touched the ground Bennett clambered out of the cockpit and slid along the top of the fuselage down to the tail-plane. His weight

3   Kuala Lumpur.

dropped the tail down quickly, with the result that the machine pulled up in about one hundred yards after touching the ground.

The next day was December 5th, and to reach Australia within the specified thirty-day time limit meant that we had to arrive in Darwin on the 12th, eight days from now, and four more landings to make after leaving Singapore. Thus it will be seen we still had four days in hand. I therefore decided to remain the whole of the next day at Singapore and work on our machine.

We now had, roughly, 2,500 miles to complete, and in all that distance I knew of only five places at which a landing could be made; the rest of the country was either mountain, jungle, or swamp; so it behooved us to look well to our machine, for a single engine trouble and a forced landing away from any of these aerodromes would have ended all.

CHAPTER X

Singapore to Surabaya

The heat at Singapore was intense and, coming from the cold of the English winter, we felt it severely. After a heavy day on the machine, we were asked that night to a dance at the Tanglin Club,[1] but physical weariness compelled us to refuse.

My host, in a very persuasive manner, did his utmost to induce me to go, assuring me the dance would be over early. However, when we arrived at our machine, at daylight next morning, and were getting ready to start off, my quondam host of the night before and some of his party arrived, all still wearing evening dress. They had just come from the early dance!

As I have mentioned previously, the ground was much too small for an aerodrome, and the rain which had fallen overnight made it very heavy.

My brother and I paced over and examined the ground and discussed the best way to take off, but we were both very dubious as to whether we could get the machine into the air or would pile her up on the adjacent houses in the attempt. I taxied into the position, so as to give the maximum amount of run, and then opened the throttle full out.

---

1   Since 1865 Singapore's Tanglin Club had been a hub or social and recreational activity for British official and expatriates.

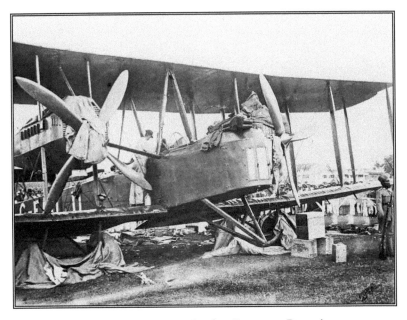

The Vimy undergoing an overhaul at Singapore, December, 1919.
[Ross and Keith Smith Collection, SLSA PRG 18/7/24]

We gathered way slowly, and I watched the fence around the course come rapidly nearer and nearer, and still we were not off the ground. It was a tense and anxious moment. When fifty yards from the rails, I pulled my control-lever back; the trusty Vimy rose to the occasion and just cleared the rails. There were still houses and trees to be negotiated, and I set the Vimy climbing at an alarming steep angle.

Another breathless moment passed, and the wheels of the under-carriage just cleared the treetops. It was a great triumph for the Vimy. She achieved the seemingly impossible, and to this day I regard our escape from disaster during this perilous take-off as providential.

After a wide sweep above Singapore, we headed for the open sea and Java. Passing down to the Sumatran coast, we ran into characteristic doldrum weather—isolated patches of dark thunderstorm clouds, from which the rain teemed down in heavy murky columns.

Occasional forks of lightning seared the clouds, throwing up into relief their immense bulk and shedding a flickering gleam over the calm sea, where almost stagnation expanded. Occasionally a light zephyr came out of the east, but almost in the course of a few minutes the puff had boxed the compass and died away.

The spectacle of these local storms was extremely uncanny, and by navigating accordingly it was easy to avoid them. On reaching the coast of Sumatra we encountered a light head wind and flying conditions became very bumpy. One immense vacuum into which we fell made us hold tight and wonder. 'That's the Equator,' ejaculated my brother, and, sure enough, by dead reckoning, we had bumped across the line into the Southern Hemisphere.

Our entrance into the Southern Hemisphere was welcomed by improved weather, but the landscape below—dense jungle inland, fringed along the seashore by belts of mangrove swamps and the blue tropical sea—often kindled in my mind thoughts of utter helplessness in case of engine trouble.

There developed in me a strange admiration—almost reverence—for the super-mechanism that hummed away rhythmically, that had now covered 10,000 miles without an overhaul, and at the opposite side of the globe was still singing a hymn of praise to the makers, as it had done when the bleak wintry snows had carpeted the aerodrome at Hounslow and Northern France. How far away this all seemed!

These were times, for musing, as we sped along above this tranquil tropical landscape, home only a few days away—an achievement!

Numerous small islets—emeralds in a setting of turquoise—
passed below us. There were yearnings to land and explore their
mangrove-fringed bays and foreshores, but the nearest landing
ground was our destination, Batavia.

Soon the large island of Muntok[2] came below, and in the strait
separating the mainland we passed a vessel. Subsequently we learned
she was equipped with wireless and had transmitted news of our
arrival on to Batavia.

I had originally intended to hug the coast of Sumatra on to Java;
but as it was all dense mangrove swamp with no sign of a possible
landing place, I reasoned that we might just as well fly over the sea.
My brother computed the compass course, and so we headed direct
for Batavia.

The hazy contours of the mountains marking the western end of
Java soon began to show up to starboard, and ahead a scene of rare
enchantment began to resolve itself upon the bosom of the tropical sea.

The sea was a glorious mirror almost as rippleless as the canopy
above, and scattered broadcast lay the Thousand Isles, each one
beautiful, and all combined to make one of the most beautiful sights
I have ever looked down upon. Many of the islands are heavily grown
with palms extending to the very water's edge; others, sparsely
cultivated, fringed with a narrow ribbon of beach; but around each is
a setting of an exquisite shade of green, marking a sand-girt shallow;
then deep blue and depth.

Myriads of tiny white fisher-sails passed through the channels,
gleaning their harvest from the sea.

Reluctantly we turned from this glimpse of fairy-land, and,

---

2   Mentok is a port city on the island of Bangka or Banka off the east coast of South
    Sumatra.

bearing for the Garden Island of the East, soon reached Batavia, the city of canals and beautiful avenues.

Following the railway line, we landed at the Dutch Flying School at Kalidjati.[3] The Dutch had sent an escort of four machines to welcome us; but, although they passed within about 500 feet of the Vimy, they missed us.

The distance of 650 miles from Singapore we had covered in just nine hours. Hearty greeting was extended to us by His Excellency Count Van Limburg Stirum, the Governor-General of the Netherlands Indies, and a large number of leading officials.

Kalidjati is one of the best aerodromes I have ever seen. It is a huge place nestling at the foot of the mountains and it is no wonder that the Dutch flying officers and their mechanics are a cheery lot in such ideal surroundings.

We were treated with the greatest hospitality and kindness; nothing was too much trouble for our friends, and the Governor-General himself gave orders that we were to be the guests of his Government while passing through the Netherlands East Indies.

I was delighted to learn that several aerodromes had been constructed between Java and Australia for our use and I lost no time in expressing my heartfelt thanks to His Excellency for his kindness and the interest which he had taken in our flight, without which we never would have reached Australia within the allotted thirty days.

After a well-enjoyed meal, we set to work on the machine. The petrol available was very heavy, and it took us six hours to filter 350 gallons through the chamois leather strainer into the tanks. As the

---

3   Or Kalijati, approximately 100 kilometres east-south-east of Batavia (Jakarta).

next stage to Surabaya was only a short lap, we did not leave Kalidjati before 7.30 am.

With beautiful weather favouring us, we sped rapidly over fertile tracts of this amazing island, charmed by the unsurpassable beauty that unfolded below. Java impressed me as one vast bounteous garden, amid which rise the immense, shapely cones of volcanic mountains.

Perhaps one of the most striking sights was the 'paddy' country. From our height, the whole expanse of the land appeared to be inundated by irrigation water—all contained in minute, cell-like squares, that gave the effect of a mighty grid, stretching away to the mountains on our right. Even there the irrigation did not cease, but climbed up the mountain sides in a system of stair-like terraces.

Here and there native villages nestled beneath the shelter of the palm groves or among the verdant green of sugar plantations. Always in the background, subdued by tropical haze, rose the chain of peaks, practically all quiescent, and far away to the left that faint blue line which marked the Pacific horizon.

Nearing Surabaya, flying became very bumpy, and it was no small relief when the town, like a magic carpet of multi-coloured fabric, spread beneath us. Heading the Vimy down, we made a low circle above the town, to the infinite amazement of the teeming native population that swarmed out into the streets, petrified, evidently, by the visitation.

From above, the surface of the aerodrome on which we were to land appeared to be ideal, but the whole ground was somewhat small. I landed along the south side intending to open up one engine and swing the machine round on the ground if there appeared any danger of over-shooting and running into a bank of earth at the end. This manoeuvre, however, I discovered to be unnecessary. We made a good landing and were easing off to rest when the machine seemed to drag, and from past experience I knew at once the Vimy was becoming bogged.

Opening up the starboard engine, we began to swing slowly, but the port wheels immediately sank into the mud and we tilted on to our fore-skid. At once I shut off both engines and the Vimy gradually eased back to her normal position. I then discovered that our aerodrome was a stretch of land that had been reclaimed from the sea; the top crust had set quite hard, but underneath was a layer of liquid mud.

The natives and people, who had been kept back by the Dutch soldiers, rushed the ground, and their weight on the sun-dried crust soon broke it up, and mud began to ooze through. In a very short while the Vimy subsided to her axles and was surrounded by a pond of semi-liquid mud.

The proposition literally was a decidedly sticky one. It was midday, broiling hot, and the tenacity of the mud reminded me forcibly of that clinging tendency familiar to our black-soil plains. Moreover, only four days of our prescribed time remained, in which we must make Port Darwin.

The engineer of the Harbour Board arrived, and together we discussed the situation. He collected a horde of coolies and a large quantity of bamboo matting, and so we set to work to dig out the wheels. After some hard work we got the matting almost under the wheels, started up the engines and aided by the coolies and Dutch soldiers, the Vimy was hauled from the bog. I then stopped the engines, tied ropes to the under-carriage, and the machine was pulled on to a pathway of mats.

Digging out the wheels at Surabaya, Sumatra, and laying bamboo mats to
assist take off, 8 December 1919. [Photograph by John Furlong,
SLSA PRG 1701/1/3]

Digging out the Vimy utilising bamboo matting track, at Surabaya,
7 December 1919. [Ross and Keith Smith Collection, SLSA PRG 18/7/33]

After a couple of hours the machine was safe out of the morass, and the ground on which we stood felt quite solid; so I thought we had landed on the only soft spot on the aerodrome, and decided to taxi to the opposite end under our own engine-power.

I was soon disillusioned, for, after moving but ten yards, down went the wheels again. More digging, tugging, and pushing, and we, apprehensive all the while as to whether the coolies would drag off the under-carriage, finally had to lay down a pathway of bamboo mats and have the machine hauled by 200 coolie power.

We had landed at 12 noon and after six hours of hard work under a boiling tropical sun we had the Vimy on a platform of bamboo mats at the end of the aerodrome. Some of the matting had large nails sticking out of it and two of our tyres were punctured. Bennett and Shiers as usual attended the engines first, while Keith and I replenished our tanks with petrol and oil. Fortunately we did not have to put in so much petrol as usual and we then attacked the two punctured tyres. By this time it was dark, but we worked on by the light from the lamps of a motor car.

The Vimy, fully loaded, weighs about six tons, and just as we had got one wheel jacked up the ground beneath sank under the weight and the jack broke. We borrowed another jack from our friend with the motor car, but this also suffered a similar fate. We had had no food since early morning, so tired and disconsolate we decided to leave the machine for the night and resume our efforts in the morning. I don't think I have ever felt so tired or so miserable in my life as I did then. Here we were only 1,200 miles from Australia; we still had four of our thirty days left in which to do it, and yet to all intents and purposes we were hopelessly stuck in this quagmire without a chance of getting out of it. Furthermore, I knew that this was the only flat stretch of land within 400 miles from which it was possible to get the Vimy into the air. It seemed as if victory were to be snatched from us at the last moment.

But just when things were looking blackest a bright idea occurred to my brother. We knew that it would be impossible to get off this aerodrome in the usual way, but why not construct a roadway of mats to prevent our wheels sinking into the mud, then run along it and so get into the air!

Straightway we sought out the Harbour Board Engineer, but he said it would be impossible to get so many mats together in so short a time. However, after much persuasion he agreed to have as many mats as possible at the aerodrome next morning. This cheering news considerably revived our sinking spirits and we went off to our hotel in a much happier frame of mind.

The British Consul had invited us to a 'quiet little dinner' that evening, but when we arrived at the restaurant, an hour late, we found that all the British residents in Surabaya had gathered there to welcome us. It was a very happy party and a most enjoyable diversion from our efforts of the past few hours.

Next morning saw us at the aerodrome by daylight, and a gladsome sight met our eyes. Natives were streaming in from every direction bearing sheets of bamboo matting—they were literally carrying their houses on their backs—and already a great pile of it lay by the Vimy.

At first a pathway of mats was merely laid down, but in our keen anxiety to set off we had overlooked the 'slip-stream' from the propellers. The engines were opened up and we were just gathering speed nicely when some of the sheets were whisked up and blown into the tail-plane. This threw the machine out of control and to our dismay the Vimy ran off the matting and bogged again. Once more we had to dig deep down and place great planks under the wheels and haul the Vimy back into the matting. I have never been able to understand how the machine stood the rough handling she received; it speaks volumes for the material and thoroughness of her construction. Of course the coolies had no idea which parts were safe to pull and which were not and to try and watch 200 of them and get anything like team work out of them was somewhat of a problem. More matting arrived on a motor lorry, so we made the road about 300 yards long and 40 feet wide and this time pegged it all down and interlaced the mats so that they could not blow up. At last all was ready and just 24 hours after our arrival at Surabaya we started up the engines, ran along the roadway, and with feelings of intense relief felt the Vimy take off and get into the air.

We circled low over the town and anchorage, so as to give the engines time to settle down to normal running; and then headed on a direct compass course for Bima.

CHAPTER XI

Into Australia

From the point of view of a prospective forced landing, the 400-mile flight to Bima was impossible. Not a single flat occurred on which we might have landed. Scenically, this lap was glorious. We skirted the coast of Bali and Lombok, keeping 3,000 feet above the sea. Not a ripple disturbed its surface and looking over the side from time to time I could see a lot of small splashes in the water in the form of a circle. For a time these splashes puzzled me and then I caught a glint of silvery wings and knew that they were made by flying fish. My brother also had seen them and we were both rather surprised to be able to see flying fish from a height of 3,000 feet. It made me think that perhaps after all the hawks and other birds that we see flying about have not such wonderful eyesight as we imagine, because it is undoubtedly easier to see an object from the air than on the ground.

Bima aerodrome in the island of Sumbawa was in excellent condition and clearly marked with a huge white cross in the centre which we saw several miles away. The natives scampered in all directions and would not venture near until they saw us walking about the machine.

The local Sultan and the Dutch Commissioner met us and proffered the hospitality of a native bungalow a couple of miles from the machine. Here we aroused intense interest; eyes taking little furtive glimpses at us peered through every crack and gap.

During the night we were awakened to hear some fellow prowling about outside. I waited until he was opposite the doorway, then a shot from my Very light pistol put him to a screaming and, I have no doubt, a terror-stricken flight.

The natives had recovered from their shyness by next morning, and on our arrival were swarming around the machine with presents of cocoanuts sufficient to start a plantation; evidently they thought the Vimy a very thirsty sort of bird.

We took a cargo of nuts on board, as the water was unsuited for drinking, and, setting off in dazzling sunshine, once more pursued our course above scenes of tropical enchantment and alluring charm. After following the north coast of Flores to Reo,[1] we crossed over to the south side of the island and ran into isolated rainstorms. Once we saw a small active volcano in the distance and were tempted to go off and gaze down into its smoking crater, but as the weather indicated a change for the worse, we could not afford to make a deviation. We flew on as far as Pandar, and then swung off direct for Timor.

We had by this time acquired such confidence in our engines that it mattered little what lay below us—sea or land.

A thick haze soon obscured the land and all distant vision, but we eventually picked up the Timor coast a few hundred yards from our calculated position. Ten miles inland we came down on the aerodrome at Atamboea, our last landing ground before Port Darwin.

---

[1]   Reo is located on the north coast of Flores, one of the Lesser Sunda Islands.

The Dutch officials had thoughtfully arranged our petrol and oil supply close at hand, saving us a good deal of valuable time, which we were able to devote to a thorough overhaul.

Tomorrow would be the great day whereupon reposed the destiny of our hopes, labours, and ideals. This was one of the aerodromes specially made by the Governor-General of the Netherlands Indies for the Australian flight, and had been completed only the day before our arrival. A guard of Dutch soldiers kept watch over the machine while we proceeded with their officers to camp, some six miles away.

It is hardly necessary to say that none of us overslept. We were too excited at the prospect of the morrow. We felt sure that if it dawned fine and hot, our homing was assured; but as we stepped out, before sunrise, into the still, sluggish air, we realised that our hopes of an early start were small. A heavy haze lay over the sea and the coast, obscuring everything; so we decided to await its clearing.

We were at the aerodrome before sun-up to discover that a great swarm of natives were even earlier risers than ourselves. Most had come afoot, but many had ridden their ponies, and they clustered on and around the fence, behind and beside the Vimy, like swarming bees. We had hauled the machine well back with the tail against the fence in order to take advantage of every foot of the short run.

Our start-off was brightened by one of those incidents that usually make material for comic papers. The propellers were just 'kicking' over, like two great fans, and those natives sitting on the fence in the line of the slip-stream were enjoying the cool breeze and looking pleased with themselves. When I opened up the engines and both propellers swung into action, the sudden blast of air sent these particular spectators toppling back into the crowd, where ponies and natives made a glorious mix-up, at which we all laughed heartily.

If an aeroplane is forced to land in the sea it usually floats for a time, then the forward part sinks and only the tail remains above water. Remembering this, just before leaving Timor we tied a parcel of food, a bottle of water, the Very pistol[2] and some cartridges on to the tail so that we would have something to fall back upon in case of emergency.

Soon after 8 the fog began to thin, and at 8.35, to be exact, I opened up the engines and just managed to scrape out of the aerodrome. Scrape is exactly the word, for the branch-tops of the gum-tree rasped along the bottom of the machine as we rose. It was indeed one of the closest shaves of the trip.

In front of us rose a chain of high hills, and, as the atmosphere was hot and we climbed very slowly, we made a detour to avoid them. Still flying low, we approached the coast and pulled ourselves together for the final lap—the jump across the Arafura Sea that lay between us and Port Darwin.

Keith took all possible bearings, noted wind direction, and made numerous calculations of ground speeds. Then we set compass course for Darwin, and with a 'Here goes!' we were out over the sea. All our hearts were beating a little quicker; even our fine old engines seemed to throb a trifle faster.

This was to be our longest stretch over open sea and I did not relish the prospect of being out of sight of land for five hours. However, as the coastline of Timor receded and disappeared behind us, my thoughts turned back to the great transatlantic flight made by the late Sir John Alcock in a Vimy similar to our own. What had we to fear with only a few hundred miles of open sea to cross, while he had nearly 2,000?

---

2 A Very pistol is a flare gun for signalling, especially in distress.

The Australian Government had arranged that a warship should patrol the sea between Timor and Port Darwin in case we should need help, and anxiously we scanned the distant horizon for the first glimpse of her.

Our watches registered 11.48 when Keith nodded ahead, and dead on the line of flight we made out a faint smoke that soon resolved itself into the smoke plume of a fighting-ship. It was the HMAS *Sydney*, and we knew now that, whatever might befall, we had a friend at hand.

We swooped low, and exactly at twelve minutes past noon passed over the vessel, seeing plainly the upturned faces of the sailors and their waving hands. It was a cheer of welcome quite different from anything that we had experienced on the long journey. Perhaps it is not to be wondered at that the result of our snapshot was blurred through the shaking of the camera.

We took the opportunity of snatching a speed test, and found that we were averaging seventy-five miles an hour.

Two hours later both of us saw ahead and to port what appeared to be haze, but which we hoped was land, though neither dared express his hopes. They were justified, however, ten minutes later, and hailing Bennett and Shiers, we pointed joyfully to Bathurst Island lighthouse.

It was just 2.06 pm when, as our diary prosaically notes, we 'observed Australia'. At 3 o'clock we not only observed it, but rested firmly upon it, for, having circled over Darwin and come low enough to observe the crowds and the landing place, we landed on Terra Australis on December 10th, 27 days, 20 hours after taking off from Hounslow.

We had won the race against time and the £10,000 prize with just 52 hours to spare!

Two zealous customs and health officials were anxious to examine us, but so were about 2,000 just ordinary citizens, and the odds of 1,000 to 1 were rather long for those departmental men, and our welcome was not delayed.

The hardships and perils of the past month were forgotten in the excitement of the present. We shook hands with one another, our hearts swelling with those emotions invoked by achievement and the glamour of the moment. It was, and will be, perhaps, the supreme hour of our lives.

Almost reverently we looked over the Vimy, and unspoken admiration crept over us as we paid a silent tribute to those in far-off England for their sterling and honest craftsmanship. The successful issue of the venture in a great degree was due to them, and surely they merited and deserved a large proportion of the praise.

Through every possible climatic rigour the Vimy had passed, and practically without any attention. Not once, from the time we took our departure from Hounslow, had she ever been under shelter. And now, as I looked over her, aglow with pride, the Vimy loomed up as the zenith of man's inventive and constructional genius. I could find neither fault nor flaw in the construction, and, given a few days' overhaul on the engines, the Vimy would have been quite capable of turning round and flying back to England.

These reflections were of brief duration, for the crowd, having satisfied its curiosity over the machine, directed it to us. The Administrator of the Northern Territory and the Mayor of Darwin were given barely time to make an official welcome when the assemblage, brimming with enthusiasm, lifted us shoulder high and conveyed us to the jail.

Crowds of spectators gathered on 10 December 1919 to view the Vimy
at Darwin. [Photograph by John Furlong, SLSA PRG 1701/1/5]

This sinister objective for the moment gave us qualms, for we fully expected a charge of exceeding the speed limit to be preferred against us. That drastic apprehension resolved itself into being dumped on a tree-stump, historic or otherwise, in the garden, while raucous howls of 'Speech! Speech!' came from the hospitable multitude.

After the exchange of much 'hot air' on both sides, we returned to the Vimy, made all snug, and lashed her down for the night.

During our stay at Darwin we were the guests of Mr Staniford Smith, at Government House.[3] And now we were to be bewildered by an amazing array of cables and telegrams. They arrived in great fifteen-minute shoals from every corner of the globe.

What had gone wrong? Surely every one had gone mad—or had we? Why all this fuss and excitement? Since leaving London we had not read a newspaper, and, beyond the local natural attention evinced at our numerous landing grounds, we knew nothing of the interest the rest of the world was taking in the flight.

Great indeed was our astonishment when, on turning up back files of newspapers, we read of our exploits, recorded with a degree of detail that must have taxed the imaginative resources of editorial staffs to grey hairs.

The rush, strain, and anxiety were over; henceforward the conclusion of our flight across Australia could be undertaken leisurely, but we still had a distance of 3,000 miles to fly before reaching our home in Adelaide.

Our flying time from London to Darwin was 135 hours. So in the ordinary course of events we should have given our engines a top

3   Actually Staniforth Smith, himself a veteran of the Great War, and in 1919 Administrator of the Northern Territory.

overhaul—lifted the cylinders and ground in the valves, etc. This would have taken a week, and as the rainy season had just started and our aerodrome was low-lying, I was told that if we did not get off at once we would probably have to remain three months.

The port propeller was showing signs of splitting but I thought it would last until we reached Sydney where we could get another. All things considered I thought it best to get on as quickly as possible, because had we remained at Port Darwin for any length of time it is highly probable that the Vimy, standing out in the open, would have been severely damaged in one of the tropical storms that occur here frequently at this time of year.

The Minister of Defence at Melbourne had arranged petrol and oil supplies for us at various points and the first town we would reach after leaving Port Darwin was Cloncurry, in Northwestern Queensland—a distance of about 1,000 miles. The maps of all that northern part of Australia are bad and show very little detail, but we arranged to get some information about various landmarks from some stockmen who had recently returned from 'droving' a mob of cattle from Darwin to Cloncurry.

The day before we left Port Darwin, Captain Wrigley and Lieutenant Murphy of the Australian Flying Corps arrived from Melbourne in an old BE 2E machine. They had come up to meet us and had achieved a remarkable performance in having flown so far in a machine four years old. Our first mechanical troubles of the whole journey began soon after leaving Darwin. We were following the telegraph line which runs overland from Darwin to Adelaide; it was terribly hot and below us stretched a limitless expanse of undulating scrub country. After about four hours of very uncomfortable flying, valve trouble developed in the starboard engine and I decided to land on a dried-up swamp a few miles ahead. It turned out to be very rough ground, but we got down safely and Shiers soon had the engine right again. There was a good water hole at one side of the swamp and as flying conditions were so bad we decided to lay up under the shade of the wings for the rest of the day and go on early next morning. We learned afterward that the place where we had landed rejoices in the name of 'Warlock Ponds', and I am never likely to forget it as long as I live. As soon as the sun went down a solitary mosquito came buzzing around our little camp and presently selected Shiers as his victim. Finding him good, the mosquito, being a sportsman, did not wait until he had had his fill, but buzzed off back to his pals at the water hole and told them of his find. In a few minutes the air was thick with them and I have never known insects so venomous. Sleep was impossible and the only way we could rest was by wrapping ourselves completely in a blanket, but it was too hot to do this for long. We tried grass fires, a petrol fire, and everything else that we could think of, but all to no avail, and soon our faces, arms, and legs were just a mass of lumps. About midnight I suddenly remembered that I had a bottle of very good Irish whisky in the machine that had been given me in London. It had not been opened and so at last I thought I had found something to keep these pests away. The whisky was divided into four portions and at once I proceeded to splash mine all over myself while the others watched the result. It was not long in coming—I am sure those mosquitos must have thought it was Christmas; they fairly swarmed around me and then kept coming back for another drink! To add to my discomfort I was forced to watch Keith and Bennett and Shiers *drink* their portions while I vainly tried to lick up the drips that were running down my face.

It was after daylight before we managed to sleep and so our start was delayed until 10 am. If anything it was hotter than the preceding day and consequently the air was full of pockets and bumps and at times I had to work hard to keep the machine under control. We left the telegraph line at Newcastle Waters and turned off southeast. There was nothing on our map to guide us, but the stockmen in Port Darwin told us that if we flew southeast from Newcastle Waters for about 100 miles we would see two large patches of scrub which almost met each other in the form of a V. Then if we went down low, we would see the tracks of a mob of cattle that they had driven over there a few months previously. A few miles further on we would come onto a rough bush road that led on toward Cloncurry. It all came out just as they had said; we picked out the two patches of scrub and then came down and saw the tracks of the cattle. Surely this was rather a novel form of navigation.

About an hour later I was startled by a loud crack from the port propeller and was horrified to see that one blade had split from the tip to the boss. There was a tent pitched by the side of a track about a mile ahead, so I shut off both engines and came down and landed.

We calculated that we were about twenty miles away from Anthony's Lagoon where there was a small police station and a petrol depot. At first it looked hopeless to think of repairing the propeller and going on, and so here we were marooned in a dry and desolate part of Australia, 150 miles from a telegraph and 450 miles from the nearest railway. It was not a pleasing prospect by any means. Just after we landed we were greatly astonished to see two motor cars coming toward us. It seemed too good to be true, as we thought that we would certainly have to walk the twenty-odd miles to Anthony's Lagoon before we could hope for any assistance. The cars contained

Ross Smith (left), Walter Shiers (centre), and Keith Smith (right)
enjoying a meal break by the Vimy at Cobbs Creek, Northern Territory,
while mending the broken propeller, 14–17 December 1919.
[Photograph by J.M. Bennett, Ross and Keith Smith Collection,
SLSA PRG 18/7/51]

Mr Sydney Peacock and his son, and Sergeant Stretton of the Mounted Police. Mr Peacock had been sinking a sub-artesian bore just where we landed and he was now going to remove his camp and travel back into Queensland until after the summer. Had we arrived an hour later he would have struck his camp and gone and we would have been faced with a long, hot, and dry walk.

We had little food and no water in the Vimy, but Mr Peacock kindly insisted on leaving us all his before he departed, and he arranged to have supplies sent out to us from Anthony's Lagoon. He also left us a sheet of galvanized iron with which Bennett said he could mend the broken propeller. We were camped there for three and a half days, during which time Sergeant Bennett carried out a wonderful, and what I consider, a unique piece of skilful workmanship. When the propeller blade had split in the air several splinters of wood had flown off, but Bennett, nothing daunted, shaped new bits out of a piece of packing case to fill the gaps. He next glued the split portions together, then cut the sheet of galvanized iron into strips and bound them round the blade. The strips of iron were fastened onto the blade with screws which we had taken out of the floor boards of the machine. When this was done the whole blade was covered with fabric and painted.

So that there would be little or no vibration the opposite blade of the propeller had to be treated in exactly the same manner.

The conditions under which we worked were very trying and during the middle of the day it was impossible to do anything except lie in the shade of the wings and pant. The shade temperature underneath the wings was as high as 125° and the heat even melted our 'Triplex' goggles and wind screens.

Water was very scarce and none of us washed for the whole

three and a half days. The bore which Mr. Peacock had put down contained semi-brackish water and we had to haul it up 150 feet in a small bucket. It was very dirty too as the bore had not been cleaned out since it was made and the water made all of us ill when we drank it. During the day we wore no clothes except our overalls and boots, but we were really quite happy by ourselves with no one to worry us and ask the same old innumerable questions about the speed of the machine, its weight, where we sat and so forth; it was the first real rest that we had had. Keith amused me very much one evening. We were having our usual meal of tinned meat and biscuits when he suddenly remarked: 'If we had some ham, we would have some ham and eggs, if we had some eggs.' I believe it is a very old joke, but I had never heard it before and it sounded so very funny away out there, and I remember laughing about it for a long while afterward.

During the second night we were camped here a heavy thunderstorm passed over and we managed to collect quite a lot of water as it ran off the planes.

It was a great relief when the propeller was finally fitted on the engine again and so well had Bennett done his work that there was practically no vibration when the engine was running.

From Anthony's Lagoon much of the flight over featureless country would have been drear and monotonous, but it was Australia and that was compensation enough. Moreover, we had the occasional diversion of passing over small outback towns, where many of the inhabitants rushed into the streets and stood looking up, waving and cheering, and wherever we landed there was always a warm welcome awaiting us.

At Charleville in Central Queensland both engines were given a much-needed and thorough overhaul and a new propeller was made by the Queensland Government at their Railway workshop at Ipswich. It was here also that we were joined by my old friend, Captain Frank Hurley, of Antarctic fame; he completed the rest of the flight with us in the Vimy, taking films and photographs, and his cheery optimism and unfailing good humour made us all wish that he had been with us the whole way from England.

The sublimest spectacle of the entire flight from Hounslow to our journey's end was to burst upon us when we arrived over Sydney and its wonderful harbour.

Like a mighty fern-leaf, ramifying and studded with islets, this glorious waterway unfolded below. The city and its environs, massed along the waterfront and extending into the hinterlands, flanked by the Blue Mountains, compose a spectacle of exquisite charm and beauty.

We headed up the coast and, turning through the entrance, entered the port.

Flying into Sydney at the end of their journey, over the Harbour.
[Ross and Keith Smith Collection, SLSA PRG 18/9/1/38D]

The crew, Ross Smith, Keith Smith, James Bennett, and Walter Shiers, flying into Sydney on 14 February 1920. [Photograph by Frank Hurley. Ross and Keith Smith Collection, SLSA PRG 18/7/59]

Planing down to 600 feet, we flew above a myriad ferry-boats and vessels, from the whistles of which little white jets of steam spurted up, screaming a welcome; then across the roof-tops, where crowded waving and cheering humanity, and over the streets below, where little specks paused to look up and join in the greeting. It was a great day—a time that comes once in a lifetime.

Ross (left) and Keith Smith (right) reunited with their parents Jessie and Andrew Smith, 14 February 1920, after landing at Mascot, New South Wales. [Photograph by Arthur Martin, Ross and Keith Smith Collection, SLSA PRG 18/7/66]

Crowds surrounding the Vickers Vimy and crew at Mascot, New South Wales.
14 February 1920. [Ross and Keith Smith Collection, SLSA PRG 18/7/61]

Vickers Vimy crew meeting Prime Minister Hughes, 27 February 1920. In the centre of the photograph, left to right: James Bennett, Ross Smith, Prime Minister William Morris Hughes, Keith Smith, Andrew Smith, Walter Shiers. [Ross and Keith Smith Collection, SLSA PRG 18/7/72]

Not the least pleasant incident upon our arrival finally in Melbourne was the paying over of the £10,000 prize by the Prime Minister, the Right Hon. W.M. Hughes, on behalf of the Commonwealth Government. As all participated equally in the perils and labors of the enterprise, the prize was divided into four equal shares.

In Melbourne I formally handed the Vimy over to the Commonwealth Government on behalf of Messrs Vickers Ltd, who generously presented the machine to the Commonwealth as an historic relic of the first aerial flight from London to Australia. At the request of the authorities, I flew the machine on to Adelaide, my native city, and thus realised to the full my ambition and dream of flying from London to my own home.

It would be hard indeed to comprehend the feelings that surged through me as I landed the Vimy on the sod of my native city—the recognition of familiar faces; the greeting of well-known voices; the hand-clasp of innumerable friends; but, greatest of all, the reunion with my parents after five long years.

Our heartfelt thanks are due to the officers and mechanics of the Royal Air Force; to the Dutch authorities for constructing aerodromes and other assistance, and for the cooperation of numerous friends, whose willing and generous help laid the paving-stones over which Fortune piloted me.

My brother Keith shares equally any worthiness that the effort might merit, as also do my two master mechanics, Sergeants Bennett and Shiers, whose loyalty and devotion to duty have done much to bind closer the outposts of the Empire through the trails of the skies.

Ross Smith at Parliament House, Adelaide, on the day the Vimy landed.
[Ross and Keith Smith Collection, SLSA PRG 18/7/76]

The end of the great flight—the crowd welcoming the Vickers Vimy and crew
in Northfield, Adelaide on 23 March 1920. Mounted police are supervising the
crowd and there are spectators standing on top of the building on the right,
with signage for 'The Harry J. Butler & Kauper Aviation Co. Ltd'.
[Photograph by Frank Hurley. SLSA PRG 18/16/27.]

Ross and Keith Smith leaving Buckingham Palace in 1921
after being knighted as members of the Order of the British Empire
(KBE) by King George V, in recognition of their flight.
[Ross and Keith Smith Collection, SLSA PRG 18/10/3]

Sir Ross Smith standing alongside the plane in which he was to lose his life,
a Vickers Viking amphibian in a factory at Weybridge, England.
[Ross and Keith Smith Collection, SLSA PRG 18/13/3]

Portrait of Sir Ross Smith, in Air Force uniform,
by William Beckwith McInnes, painted 1920.

[Ross and Keith Smith Collection, SLSA PRG 18/1/25]

The Home of the Blizzard

An Australian hero's classic tale of Antarctic discovery
and adventure

SIR DOUGLAS MAWSON

The Home of the Blizzard is a tale of discovery and adventure, of pioneering deeds, great courage, heart-stopping rescues and heroic endurance. This is Mawson's own account of his years spent in sub-zero temperatures and gale-force winds. At its heart is the epic journey of 1912–13, during which both his companions perished. Told in a laconic but gripping style, this is the classic account of the struggle for survival of the Australasian Antarctic Expedition – a journey which mapped more of Antarctica than any expedition before or since.

The photographs included in this book were taken on the journey by Frank Hurley, later to achieve fame on Sir Ernest Shackleton's *Endurance* expedition.

For more information please visit www.wakefieldpress.com.au

Long Flight Home

LAINIE ANDERSON

Wally Shiers meets Helena Alford when he happens on a couple of kids throwing eggs at the house where she lives with her mother and brother. It's 1914, and Helena's family is German. Soon, Wally will find himself fighting in Egypt and Palestine, while Helena campaigns for conscription at home – and waits for him to return to marry her.

But at the end of the war, Wally puts their wedding on hold to join Captain Ross Smith in the adventure of a lifetime, the record-breaking Great Australian Air Race – and the long flight home. Will Helena forgive him for putting his ambitions on the world stage ahead of their dreams of a shared future?

Journalist Lainie Anderson re-imagines the race through the eyes of real-life aviation mechanic Wally Shiers, bringing this rip-roaring adventure to life through a blend of immaculate research, vivid imaginative detail, and an absorbing romance that feels utterly contemporary.

2019 marks the centenary of the Great Australian Air Race, in which the Australian government offered 10,000 pounds for the first successful flight from Great Britain to Australia in under 30 days.

For more information please visit www.wakefieldpress.com.au

Wakefield Press is an independent publishing and
distribution company based in Adelaide, South Australia.
We love good stories and publish beautiful books.
To see our full range of books, please visit our website at
www.wakefieldpress.com.au
where all titles are available for purchase.
To keep up with our latest releases, news and events,
subscribe to our monthly newsletter.

Find us!

Facebook: www.facebook.com/wakefield.press
Twitter: www.twitter.com/wakefieldpress
Instagram: www.instagram.com/wakefieldpress

Lightning Source UK Ltd.
Milton Keynes UK
UKHW040636210222
398996UK00002B/120